MY ELECTRIC BOATS

CHARLES A. MATHYS

Netcam Publishing
Naples, Florida

ISBN: 978-0-9843775-2-7
LCCN: Pending

Contribution acknowledgments

Inside Graphics/Photos: by the author, unless otherwise indicated.

Dedication

For all the do-it-yourselfers who tackle tasks from plumbing to high tech projects with limited resources but with great ingenuity, enormous energy and plenty of common sense. They are the doers of the world who get the jobs done for our continued progress towards a higher standard of living.

Acknowledgements

Many people helped me make this book possible. I sincerely thank, first of all, my wife, Marjorie, who let me play with my boats and motors rather than attend to the many household chores that were of much greater importance. I also thank my friends, Bob Spettle, Bob McKelvie, George Nelson and Aaron Knott for their many helpful suggestions and comments when they reviewed the manuscript. As well as my long time friend, Don Leary, who reviewed the early material and helped me organize the book.

I am also indebted to the many business owners who spent a good deal of time educating me in the practical aspects of motor characteristics, rewinding and testing. Among them are Morton Ray owner of Ray Electric Outboard Co, Bob Sandman of Sandman Electric Co. and Joe Horvath who owns the motor rewinding shop in Naples, Florida.

Glossary of Technical Terms

***Ampere:** a measure of the current (the number of electrons) flowing in an electrical wire

Anti-ambiguity circuit: in the context used here, a circuit which prohibits 2 switches from closing at the same time

Battery Taps: the connections between batteries in a battery pack such as at the 12 and 24 volt levels

Commutator: the rotating electrical switch in a DC motor which selects the field winding to be energized

Coupler: device used to connect two shafts together

Cross-talk: electric noise created in adjacent wires

Dynamometer: device used to measure the amount of power developed by an electric motor

Force: the amount of push or pull applied to an object

Integrated Circuit (also known as an "IC" or a "Chip"): an electronic device made up from a large number of transistors

Inverter: Device which changes DC to AC

Horsepower: mechanically equal to 550 foot–pounds of force per second. Electrically equal to 746 watts

Hull speed: speed of a boat equal to the square root of the water line distance in feet times 1.3

Knot: measure of speed equal to 1.15 times the speed in miles per hour

Logic (Board): electronic circuit board containing integrated circuits and other electronic devices

Millivolt: one thousandth of a volt

Mosfet: electronic switching device used to generate the square waves which power an AC motor

Planing Hull: type of boat hull which skims over the water

Poles: as used in this book, they are the connections to a switch, relay or solenoid used to start and reverse the motor

Relay: mechanical switching device to start/stop or reverse the direction of a motor

Shunt: device inserted in an electrical circuit to measure current flow in amperes
Snubber: electronic device used to absorb unwanted destructive pulses
Solenoid: same as a relay
Spline: matching grooves or serrations near the end of shafts to be coupled together
Three Phase AC: Most common method of transmitting electricity. Three wires conduct three interlaced 60 cycle, single phase electrical sources spaced 120 degrees apart
Torque: Rotating moment of force. For example, as is applied when tightening a bolt
Transistor: semi-conductor device used to switch or amplify electronic signals, basic building block of integrated circuits.
***Volt:** the voltage across a conductor when one ampere is flowing in a conductor with a resistance of one ohm, dissipating one watt of power. Volt=amp x ohm
***Watt:** Rate of work done when one ampere flows through a differential of one volt. Watt = volt x amp
X-Y Axis: The many graphs in this book show the relation of two variables as they affect one another.
For example: Figure 1.1 shows how the speed of the boat (on the horizontal or x axis) increases when the power to the motor (on the vertical or y axis) increases.
Another common graph such as Figure 5.1 shows the results of dynamometer tests where the efficiency (y axis) changes as the power to the motor increases as shown on the x axis
***Definition of Electrical Terms**: for readers new to electrical terms, an excellent book on the basics of electricity is Miner Brotherton's "*The 12 Volt Bible for Boats*". The book can be ordered by Googling the author's name. A free download of the first 20 pages from Google Books might suffice: the information covers the terms used here, Ohm's law, and also provides an analogy of water to electricity.

Preface to the Second Edition

There were many reasons to write a second edition of "Electric Propulsion for Boats" but the main driver was to incorporate the suggestions of the reviewers and critics of the original book. The comments recommended the simplification of the technical aspects of the motor design. Although I still believe strongly that the AC motor has the best characteristics for boating applications, I have reduced its scope from 6 chapters to the single Chapter 9 which is long and still fairly technical in nature.

The year after I completed the original book I put together all the efficient components discussed at length in the first edition: namely an efficient hull, a Lynch/Etek motor and an inboard drive. This combination of components provided, by far, the best results of any configurations with which I experimented. Chapter 6, "*Sunny II* a Rhodes 19", is devoted to the design of this configuration as well as to the tests results obtained.

Much progress has been made in the field of batteries since the advent of the hybrid cars. I discuss the latest information about nickel metal hydride and lithium ion batteries. I compare the new batteries to the lead acid batteries while being mindful of the boating application involved. I also discuss the characteristics of some new motors that have been developed in the last few years.

The book is divided into 3 parts:

Part 1: Four Electric Boat Conversions
Part 2: Electric Boat Theory and Testing
Part 3: Four "Build it Yourself Projects"

I hope that this version of the book will be enjoyable to read while providing all the information needed to learn about the many aspects of electric propulsion for boats.

Introduction

First Steps

I started thinking about electric propulsion for boats about sixteen years ago. At the time, I owned an O'Day 20 ft sailboat. Knowing that an efficient hull was needed to propel the boat with as little power as possible, I decided to use the O'Day sailing hull to test the idea. The simplest solution was to buy an electric trolling motor and to put the two 12 volt batteries in series to provide 24 volts of power. At 30 amps, the input power to the motor was 720 watts or nearly 1 hp. (1 hp equals 746 watts.)

The results were under-whelming: at full power the boat moved at possibly 2 or 3 mph and lost steerage whenever the wind picked up. To a retired engineer, who loves everything about boats and has time on his hands, the seed of a challenge had been planted. After all, 1 hp was the equivalent of 7 "manpower" and you would think that 7 rowers pulling hard could move a small boat fairly fast while keeping it under control. So, the question was how much power was needed to move a small boat at hull speed and could that amount of power realistically be generated electrically?

The answer is that 1 to 2 hp is adequate to achieve hull speed in a small sailboat.

One way to prove this statement is to consider the power developed by the sails. In Thomas Firth Jones' book *Low Resistance Boats*, he quoted Bill Durham: "One thousand square feet of modern sails will reliably deliver 1 hp (running in a 10 knot breeze) to 9 hp (reaching in a 20 knot wind)." But, said Jones, "A thousand square feet of sails would have to be put on a 45 foot boat." Interpolating the 9 hp number for a

20 foot boat with 175 square feet of sails, we find that the sails generated about 1.5 hp in a very strong wind.

Another way to prove this important premise was to consider the actual power that an outboard motor generated to move the boat forward. My 20 footer had a 6 hp Johnson outboard mounted on a bracket. The specifications state that the motor delivered the 6 hp at the output shaft at 5000 to 6000 rpm. Although I never took actual measurements, I estimated that the 80% cruising rpm needed for a comfortable 6 mph hull speed was about 4000 rpm. As we will find out later, propeller speed versus output power is a cube function. This means that as the speed of the prop increases, the power output increases much faster. In fact, when the speed of the prop is doubled, the power output increases by a factor of eight. So, at 80% of maximum rpm, the shaft hp of this outboard was approximately 3.2 hp. When this number is multiplied by the efficiency of the propeller, which could be no more than 50% considering its high speed and small diameter, we found that the actual force pushing the boat was 1.6 hp.

A third way to test the important concept that 1 to 2 hp is sufficient to move a 20 foot sailboat at hull speed was to measure the pull of the sails with the boat tied to a mooring and to compare the answer with the push produced by an electric motor. I tried this experiment and found that the biggest gust of wind on a day with 15 to 20 mph winds produced a pull of 105 lbs. I estimated that the average pull was 50 to 60 lbs. (Should someone want to try this maneuver, be sure to use a preventer on the boom because violent boat movements are likely to occur). I performed many such "static thrust" tests, where the transom of the boat was secured to a mooring and the pull of the motor was measured. One static thrust test performed with a golf cart motor powering an outboard motor leg produced 70 lbs of thrust with an input power of 1500 watts or about 2 hp. This was more thrust than the average pull of the sails on a very windy day as described above.

The fallacy demonstrated in the trolling motor experiment was that the 720 watts that we measured was the input power. The output power, which actually pushes the boat along, consists of the input power multiplied by the efficiency of the motor and of the propeller. Assuming 60% efficiency for that particular motor and 50% efficiency for that particular propeller (I am being generous on both counts), we now have 720 x 0.6 x 0.5 = 216 watts or less than 0.3 hp pushing the boat. More than two thirds of the input power was wasted in heat, friction and turbulence that did nothing to move the boat forward. In terms of "manpower," we only had 2 rowers pulling hard instead of 7. No wonder the boat moved at such a slow speed and lost maneuverability when the wind picked up.

The Need for Efficiency

A recurring theme in this book is the need for the best possible efficiency. The three major components, the hull, the motor and the propeller, all have to be selected to provide the best possible performance within the framework of a practical vessel that is fun to use. We tried to pursue this search for high efficiency without going overboard...so to speak.

A long narrow hull, like that of a racing scull or a canoe, requires far less power to propel it through the water than today's best sailboat design but it is not practical for pleasure boating. At the turn of the century, when gas engines were first installed in boats, the engines had a single cylinder and produced about 2 hp. To makeup for the lack of power, the hulls had a very long waterline and were very narrow to the point, it was said, that the passengers had to part their hair in the middle to keep the boat balanced!

The type of motor used in electric boats today is the series-wound traction motor. It isn't all that different from the motors built 100 years ago. It is very reliable and in the 2 or 3 hp size, such as the ones found in golf carts, the efficiency is about 75%. It should be pointed out, however, that 75% is the full power efficiency; at less than full power the efficiency diminishes rapidly. The performance of electric boats could be greatly improved with a more efficient electric motor for boating applications. We will see that a 3 phase AC (alternating current) motor is safer, even more reliable and more efficient than the DC (direct current) traction motor and that with appropriate electronics it can be made to run on DC batteries.

The selection of an appropriate propeller is also vital to good overall performance. It is well known that a large, slow turning propeller is more efficient than a small propeller turning at high speed. The rule is that the efficiency of the propeller continues to improve up to the point where its diameter reaches 1/3 of the boat's beam measurement at the waterline and turns at a very slow speed of 300 to 400 rpm. But in small boats, there are simply too many restrictions impeding the use of such a large propeller. And today's high-speed motors, both gas and electric, make propeller speeds in the 400 rpm range very difficult to attain. But even if we can't achieve perfection, a lot can be done to maximize performance. For example, if the efficiency of each of the three main components--the hull, the motor and the drive--could be improved by 20%, the overall improvement in terms of range would be close to double. An additional bonus comes from the battery when it is discharged slowly.

Improving the efficiency of these components is the challenge. The rest of the book describes how to meet this challenge.

Electric Cars vs. Electric Boats

Billions of dollars have been spent on the development of electric cars over the last few years without much success. The challenges are enormous: range, acceleration and hill climbing ability have to match what we've come to expect from a gas-powered car. With lead acid batteries it can't be done. The reason is simple: to store equal amounts of energy, the lead acid battery weighs about 50 times as much as gasoline (after the efficiency of the gasoline engine and that of the electric motor have been properly factored into the equation). Accordingly, to obtain a range of 300 miles, the gas powered car would require about 80 lbs of fuel while the electric car would need 4000 lbs of batteries.

Fortunately, the challenges are far less demanding for electric boats. There are no hills to climb, acceleration is not a factor and power-robbing accessories such as heat and air conditioning units are not needed. Moreover, the weight of the batteries has a minor effect on performance. In a sailboat, for instance, the batteries can replace all or part of the ballast, in which case there is no ill effect whatsoever on performance.

Types of Boats

Boats come in all sizes, shapes and prices. Their uses range from exercising in a rowboat, to fishing, to competitive sailing, to exploring. Most boats are used for fishing, day cruising or sailing in small crafts (18 to 22 feet long). Unlike cars, boats receive very little use. On average, motorboats run less than 100 hours per season and sailboats are used less than one day per week. The boating that I do fits in this average category and so do the boats that I converted to electric power.

Performance Expectations

The main criteria of performance in the context of electric boats are speed and range. There are a few electric racing boats where the hull is designed to plane, but for pleasure boating, we are limited to hull speed. Hull speed is generally understood to equal the square root of the boat's waterline dimension times a factor as high as 1.3, depending on the boat. In my experience, the power required for speeds beyond the square root of the water line figure goes up so dramatically that it is best not to plan on it in an electric boat. For example, if the boat has an 18 ft waterline, the hull speed equals the square root of the waterline or 4.25 knots (4.9 mph). We should limit our expectations to a cruise speed of 5.5 mph to avoid being disappointed.

When it comes to range, unless the boat is a sailboat where the motor is used only to set the sails and to travel to the mooring or slip, the batteries should be selected to provide six hours of running time. For example, eight standard golf cart batteries, weighing about 510 lbs and costing about $600.00, will provide 48 volts for 220 ampere hours. If the motor draws 30 amps, which is the input power of a 2 hp motor, the battery power will last more than six hours. Of course, it takes an efficient hull and an efficient drive to obtain the desirable 5 knot hull speed. A bigger boat or a less efficient one would require more batteries or would have a shorter range; that's the trade-off.

Advantages of Electric Power

For people living near a body of water where restrictions forbid the use of gas-powered outboards, the use of electric power is an attractive alternative. Mort Ray, who owns the Ray Electric Outboard Co., told me he has a large concentration of sales near Baltimore where fishing is allowed in the reservoirs but only electric powered boats are permitted.

Many people are environmentalists. They conserve energy, recycle materials and refuse to pollute the air or the waterways. For them, electric power is another way to protect the environment. If you've ever run a small outboard motor in a barrel of water and seen the scum that it leaves after a very short time, you will surely agree that it is the dirtiest internal combustion engine going.

Electric motors start instantly and the quiet, odorless and vibration-free power is a very pleasant experience. This is especially true for sailors who enjoy a quiet sail. Personally, I can't deny that engineering curiosity had a lot to do with my involvement with electric boats. However, I do like the instant and quiet power, and I am quite willing to put up with the shortcomings of limited power and the trouble of keeping the batteries charged. I hope that other technically interested, do-it-yourself boating buffs will gain some knowledge from the information that I present here and will carry it to a higher level for the benefit of those who find that there is absolutely nothing in the world better than messing about in boats.

Table of Contents

Part 3—Build It Yourself Projects

LIST OF FIGURES

LIST OF PHOTOS

PART 1

Four Electric Boat Conversions

CHAPTER 1

The O'Day 20 & Other Boats

Year One

Over a period of almost fifty years, I've owned at least twenty-five boats of various shapes and sizes, equally divided between sail and power. I built my first boat from a kit. It was an 11 ft runabout powered by a used 10 hp souped-up Mercury outboard. It was very fast, very noisy and very wet. That first summer, I trailered it to a beach, where my mother and a lady friend were spending a few days. I wanted to treat them to a ride in my new boat. Going with the waves, the ride was quite enjoyable, but on the return trip, going against the wind, we were raising sheets of water, which flew right over the windshield onto my passengers in the rear. Apparently my mother, who was a non-stop talker, swallowed quite a bit of seawater because she came down with a serious stomach disorder the next day. When I asked her why she didn't spit out the water, she said that she was afraid to spit out her dentures!

My largest boat was a 37 ft Egg Harbor which I owned with two partners for two years. It was one of the very last wooden boats made by Egg Harbor. It had all the options available, including two large international truck engines that burned fuel as if it were free. After the experience with the gas guzzling, high maintenance motorboat, I decided to try a fiberglass sailboat.

I kept the sailboat at a slip at Constitution Marina in Boston Harbor where the resident mechanic told me a strange tale about the fate of a 26 ft Chris-Craft cabin cruiser. The Chris had been brought in for a tune-up and was tied to a barge which was used as a floating machine and repair shop.

Overnight the barge sank and dragged the Chris down with it. The owner collected the insurance and the boat could be bought "as is, where is" from the insurance company. The mechanic said that he had made a bid for it and had a plan to bring the boat to the surface. This fellow was not the world's most dependable person, but he did buy the boat. His diving friend brought it to the surface by attaching several fifty-five gallon drums to it. The mechanic took the engine out and "pickled" it in kerosene. Then he pumped out the boat and most of the mud that had accumulated in its six month stay at the bottom of Boston Harbor.

At this point, he evidently ran out of ambition. Two months later, the battery that he had removed from its case was still sitting on the deck. Always on the lookout for a boating bargain, I told him I was interested in the boat and that I was looking for a good winter project. We soon made an agreement that he would store the boat for the winter and would replace the engine in the boat after I rebuilt it. I christened my new boat "Bottoms Up."

The first indication of the trouble to come was the exposed gear of the windshield motor: the white metal surrounding it had disintegrated. Upon closer examination, I found that most of the important parts made of white metal such as the carburetor and distributor had also disintegrated. The winter project turned into an expensive full year project. I also learned how to install an engine and align a drive shaft because the mechanic had vanished when it came time to perform those jobs.

Yet, "Bottoms Up" turned out to be my favorite powerboat. She had a certain scent about her that wasn't too appealing and the reverse gear (that I should have rebuilt) was always a bit temperamental, but she was a fun boat; I hated to part with her. Somehow you get attached to something that you save from extinction.

My favorite sailboat had to be the 17 ft O'Day Daysailer. I owned three of them over the years. I modified one of these boats by installing a 5 hp, four-cycle lawnmower engine coupled to the lower unit of a 5 hp outboard under the rear deck (the early Daysailers had a deck). This was long before Outboard Marine came out with a similar arrangement called the Saildrive. It worked very well except for the noise and vibration that an air-cooled engine makes at high rpm. I could never baffle the noise well enough to make cruising in that boat a pleasant experience.

A simple modification to the mast of my last Daysailer enabled it to separate right after the point where the stays were tied into the mast. That worked well; the end of the mast could be removed and secured for trailering without disconnecting the boom or the mast. I decided to buy a bigger boat mainly because the seats of the Daysailer were too uncomfortable for an older adult. Before the design of the cockpit floor was changed to make the boat self-bailing, the seats were much more comfortable. (One more example of a design trade-off that does not benefit everyone.)

The Electric Drive
The 20 ft O'Day

My 20 ft O'Day was about fifteen years old when I did the electric outboard testing. It had a short 15 inch keel suitable for trailering and for sailing in the shallow waters of Cape Cod where I kept it on a mooring. It was not fast. The hull was built more like a pointed bathtub and the sails were pretty well blown out. But it was easy to handle and I could always run it up on a nearby beach to take a break from sailing.

As I mentioned in the introduction, the idea of using a trolling motor, even the most powerful one available at the time, produced very disappointing results. Although I wanted to pursue the electric power idea, I didn't want to commit much money to it, so I looked around for really cheap parts to put an electric outboard together.

I found an old 1959, 15 hp Johnson with a blown-out power head that looked as if it weren't too corroded to take apart. I located a fellow who repaired golf carts and had recently been evicted from his location. For about $200.00, I came away with an excellent quality "Baldor" golf cart motor, an old fashioned speed controller (which consisted of three heavy duty resistors, four relays and a control switch), and six 6 volt batteries which were old but still held a charge.

In retrospect, I would have been better off with a 5 or 6 hp motor that was not as heavy and had a lower unit with a higher reduction ratio than the 15 hp's 1.75 to 1 ratio. At that point, I was learning as I went along.

Connecting an electric motor to the leg of an outboard is a fairly straightforward job. A detailed explanation is included in Chapter 13, in the "Build It Yourself" Part 3. The power head of the outboard must be replaced with the electric motor. The mounting bracket of the outboard is needed but the water pump and the shift can be discarded. Instead of the shift mechanism, a simple bracket (described in step 2) can be built to make sure that the shifting mechanism stays locked in "forward."

To attach the electric motor to the outboard leg, an adapter plate must be built. It must have four mounting holes to match the four mounting holes of the electric motor and four or five holes to match the power head mounting holes of the outboard. I've built quite a few of these since the first one and I find that a quarter inch aluminum plate does the job nicely. The interface template is described in Chapter 13.

Photo 1.1 Golf Cart Motor Outboard

To connect the shaft of the electric motor to the shaft of the outboard, a flexible coupler such as the "Lovejoy" can be used. A good thing about this coupler is that the two sections can be purchased separately to accommodate shafts of different diameters without having to buy two couplers.

The shaft of the outboard is very close to the forward wall of the leg, much too close to accommodate the two inch diameter coupler. The top front part of the leg has to be ground away to clear this interference.

Very careful measurements must be taken in two areas. The ends of the two shafts must come very close to the coupling spider. That's the rubber or plastic insert located between the two sections of the coupler. It is critical to make sure that the two shafts are correctly aligned with each other. I describe a couple of methods to accomplish this alignment as well as a better coupler than the "Lovejoy" in Chapter 13. It requires some machine work and welding, which is more expensive, but a better engineering solution. My first electric drive is shown in Photo 1.1.

Testing the First Electric Drive

As the picture shows, this electric outboard was large and heavy: it weighed about 85 pounds. Later designs used the legs of 4 hp and 5 hp outboards, which are smaller and lighter. These outboards have another advantage: the lower unit reduction ratio is greater than 1.75 to 1 ratio of the 15 hp leg.

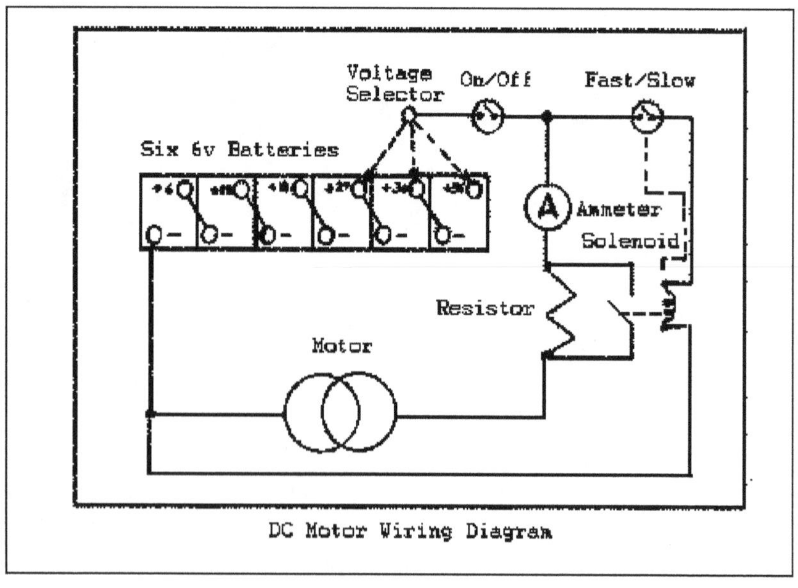

DC Motor Wiring Diagram

For testing purposes, I built a very simple controller, with two forward speeds: full speed and low speed. As the diagram above shows, the 36-volt battery is connected to a "shunt" (A) (which is a device to measure the current) and to the motor through a resistor.

The contacts of a solenoid (same thing as a relay) are connected across this resistor. The solenoid is activated by the "fast/slow" switch. When the solenoid is picked up (activated), the resistor is bypassed and the motor runs at full speed. When the solenoid is dropped out (turned off), the resistor is in series with the battery, which causes the motor to run at a slower speed. These devices had to be, of course, of the correct value and have the correct duty factor to give good results. I used the parts that came with the golf cart motor and encountered no problems.

The diagram also shows that, for test purposes, lower speeds could also be obtained by tapping the battery at lower voltages such as at 30 volts or 24 volts. When the speed is reduced by using the battery taps, none of the power supplied by the battery is wasted **but when a series resistor is used to reduce the speed, as much as 40% of the battery power is turned into heat and consequently wasted**.

Test Results from the First Electric Drive

After checking out the operation of the electric outboard in a barrel, I was ready for in-the-water tests. The first test (conducted in July of '94) was very encouraging: the operation of the motor was quiet, the boat was in complete control and seemed to have good speed.

The second time out, I picked a good day, found a willing helper, gathered some test equipment and charged the batteries. Many runs were made that day: with the wind and against the wind, with each of three propellers at three different speeds. The curves in Figure 1.1 show the results of that outing.

The battery current and the speed were measured at voltages of 24, 30 and 36 volts. By multiplying the voltage by the current, the input power was obtained in watts. For example, with 1700 watts of input power, (approximately 2.3 hp) the boat speed was about 5 knots or 5.7 mph.

Many other tests were performed with the 20 ft O'Day: static thrust tests, where the pull of the motor was measured and rpm calibrated to make sure that the speed of the motor operated in the most efficient range. **But the most important relationship, the bottom line, is always the number of watts of input power required to achieve a given speed**. This relationship is shown in Figure 1.1.

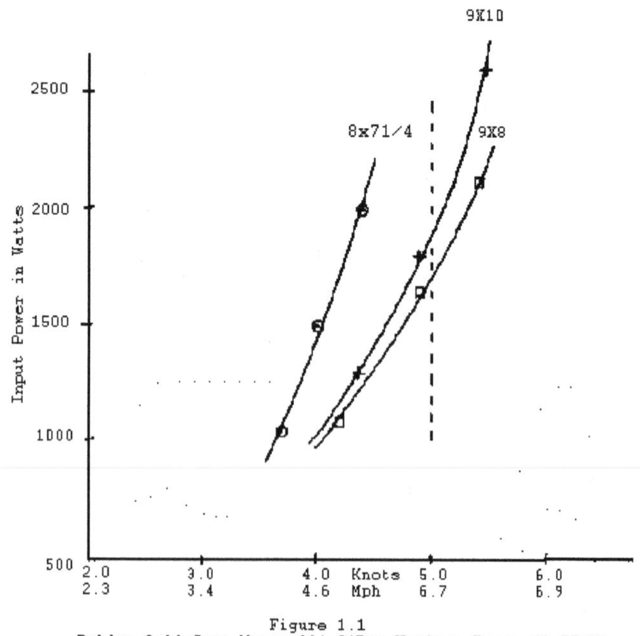

Figure 1.1
Baldor Golf Cart Motor, 20' O'Day, Various Props, (1.75/1)

Many more curves showing the speed on the x axis (across) and the power required to achieve that speed on the y axis (up and down) are found throughout the book.

Interpreting Test Results Shown in Figure 1.1

The most important test result showed that the boat ran very well at its hull speed of 5 knots with a very reasonable 1700 watts of input power. The curves shown in Figure 1.1 provide other interesting information.

It was easy to see that the 8 x 7.25 (eight inches in diameter by 7.25 inches of pitch) prop was inefficient. It required 2300 watts of power to move the boat at 5 knots, while the 9 x 8 prop required 1700 watts. Obviously, the 8 x 7.25 was the wrong prop for this boat and motor combination. It was too small in diameter, and it had too little pitch.

The other two props, both nine inches in diameter, also provided interesting insights: the prop with the ten inch pitch was equal in efficiency at less than 1000 watts, but the prop with the eight inch pitch became gradually more efficient above this level. To find the reason, the efficiency curves of the motor had to be considered. It is very likely that the motor itself became more efficient at the higher speed that the eight inch prop allowed the motor to reach. Already we can see that there is a powerful interaction between the motor and the prop in terms of efficiency. We will revisit this subject when we discuss propeller theory.

Speed vs. Power

20' O'Day with Golf-Cart Motor (1.75/1 Ratio)			
Speed in Knots	Average Input Power (Watts)	Power per Knot (Watts)	Power per Incremental Knot (Watts)
4.0	1000	250	----
5.0	1700	340	700
6.0	2500	417	800

Speed vs Power

The chart above was constructed with the data found in Figure 1.1. Column 1 shows the speed in knots. Column 2 shows the average input power to the motor using the two good propellers: the 9 x 8 and the 9 x 10. Column 3 shows how rapidly the demand for power increases as the speed increases: at 4 knots, the input power is 250 watts per knot but at 6 knots the input power jumps to 417 watts per knot. Another way to look at this phenomenon (column 4) is to observe that it takes 1000 watts to reach 4 knots but, to go one knot faster, requires an additional 700 watts. **The conclusion is that it takes an inordinately large amount of power to propel the boat beyond its hull speed, which in the case of the 20 ft O'Day is about 4.2 knots (4.8 mph).**

Off on a Tangent that Didn't Work Out

The tests performed with the 20 ft O'Day showed that the performance was about the same using a propeller with an eight inch pitch or a 10 inch pitch. I thought that it might be worthwhile to test the operation of the motor with a 1 to 1 ratio (reduction gears reduce the overall efficiency by about 4%) with less pitch on the prop to compensate for the higher prop speed. So, I built an underwater unit similar to an electric trolling motor, but I used the much more powerful Baldor golf cart motor.

Photo 1.2 The Torpedo

The device looked somewhat like a stubby torpedo (see Photo 1.2). I thought that the advantage gained by eliminating the reduction gear would make up for the loss of efficiency due to the higher rpm of the prop.

I was also intrigued by the perfect cooling effect of the water on the submerged motor. I envisioned a much smaller motor such as an aircraft starter motor, which could run continuously instead of intermittently due to the excellent cooling effect of the water compared to air cooling.

I never carried the idea very far. Sealing the motor proved to be quite a challenge, although I knew it could be done. There are millions of well pumps that operate reliably under totally submerged conditions for years.

The results were not encouraging either. I used a prop with a pitch of 6.5 inches to match the high rpm of the motor. But it caused the motor to run too slowly to be efficient. Together these two factors reduced the efficiency enough to make me give up on the idea.

At times, I still daydream of a small 3 phase, high speed motor with a built-in 10 to 1 reduction gear turning a big prop and pushing the boat smoothly and efficiently in the water...but that's beyond my mechanical skills.

By that time, the summer of '94 had pretty well run its course; it was time to end my first year's experiments and start thinking about the next year's activities.

Lessons Learned in Year One

1. Two hp of input power (1500 watts) powered a 20 ft sailboat reliably at its hull speed of 5 mph. With 500 lbs of deep cycle batteries, the range from a full charge would be more than 30 miles or about six hours.

2. To obtain good results, the diameter and the pitch of the propeller must be optimized. The diameter should be as large as practical in order to obtain the best possible efficiency, and the pitch should allow the motor to run at its most efficient speed. The interaction between propeller, motor and boat is very difficult to assess. After the initial calculations are made, several propellers need to be tested empirically to find the optimum size.

3. During that first year, I brought the batteries home to be charged each time I used the boat because the boat was on a mooring. This kind of drudgery got old very fast. With a boat at a dock or even on a trailer, charging the batteries would not have been much of a problem. For the following season, however, I planned to find a better solution for a boat on a mooring.

CHAPTER 2

Sunny, Year Two

The New Boat *Sunny*

That fall and winter I researched and then searched for the perfect hull for electric power propulsion. After much debating, I settled on a 1970 O'Day Tempest. She was 23 feet long with a 19 ft waterline and a 7.5 ft beam. She was not exactly long and slim: built more for comfort than speed. She did have the key attribute of a low resistance hull: the rear part of the hull rose substantially from mid-ship to the transom, and the transom itself was well above the waterline. The cabin was small but the cockpit was very large.

There were two main problems. First, the boat had been sitting in the owner's yard only partially covered for a couple of winters. The snow and water had ruined the cockpit floor that had been submerged for an extended period of time. Second, she had a full keel which was not suitable for trailering. But, realizing that I would never find the perfect boat, I bought her and named her *Sunny*.

This chapter describes the changes I made to *Sunny* and the performance results I obtained during the second year of testing the electric power plant.

Repairs and Modifications

I decided to transform the racing hull into something more subdued, like a motor launch. Although I kept the mast, the emphasis would be on motoring rather than sailing. I cut out the ruined cockpit floor and cut back on the size of the rear deck, which featured a well for an outboard motor, to make room for a rear seat and a small console for wheel steering (see Photo 2.1).

Photo 2.1 Gutted Cockpit of "Sunny"

The new floor, seat and console can be seen in Photo 2.2. Later, I installed 1/2 inch by 2 inch mahogany strips over the new plywood floor. It strengthened it considerably and really spruced up the looks of the cockpit.

Photo 2.2 "Sunny"'s Cockpit Rebuilt

Putting *Sunny* on a Trailer

To make the boat trailerable, I cut the 3 ft, 1200 lb keel down to 1 ft and 300 lbs. The keel was made of cast iron. I soon discovered that there was no easy way to cut cast iron. In addition, I greatly underestimated the thickness in the middle of the keel. It turned out to be six inches thick. The cutting job took seven hours.

The loss of keel weight was partly compensated by the addition of 400 lbs of batteries secured to the cabin floor. Nevertheless, the sail plan was reduced to compensate for the reduced righting moment of the lightened keel. I settled on the sail plan of a 19 ft O'Day Mariner, which has 400 lbs of lead in the cockpit floor. In any case, I needed a smaller mainsail in order to raise the boom above the canopy which would support the solar panels.

The Solar Roof

The last major construction project was to build a roof capable of supporting the solar panels. Three 12 volt, 12 x 48 inch solar panels were required to keep the batteries charged while the boat was moored. The first flat roof that I built did nothing to enhance the beauty of the boat. Later, I rebuilt the roof for a 24 volt charging system. At the same time, I added curved panels at each end, which improved the appearance of the roof somewhat. The shade from the roof provided welcome protection from the sun but there was no getting away from it: the roof made the boat look ugly. See photo 2.3 below.

Photo 2.3 36 Volt Solar Panels in the Roof

Wheel Steering

Using most of the existing parts, I connected the new steering cable to the existing rudder arrangement. It performed flawlessly throughout the testing. The 36 volt Baldor golf cart motor that I had used the previous season on the 20 ft O'Day was installed in the well area (see Photo 2.4). It encountered an early demise when I backed over a mooring line, but most of the testing was done by that time.

Photo 2.4 Golf Cart Motor Installed in the Well

Performance Results

It is said that a motor-sailer neither sails well nor motors well. In *Sunny*'s case, she motored quite well but the sailing was lacking. Running before the wind was great. The lighter weight of the boat and the minimal keel reduced the hull resistance noticeably, providing good speed even with the smaller sails. But the keel reduction really showed up when trying to point into the wind. Some sort of centerboard arrangement with at least four square feet of area was needed to stop the side slip.

The boat came with a 6 hp outboard, which I moved to an outboard bracket to make room for the electric propulsion in the well. Having one more power source might have been overdoing it a bit, but it paid to be prepared while I was experimenting. I did run the batteries all the way down a couple of times and the second power source came in handy.

In-the-Water Test Results

Figure 2.1 is a composite of many in-the-water tests using the previous year's 15 hp motor (1.75 ratio) with the Baldor DC motor and this year's new 4 hp outboard leg (2.42 ratio) with the same Baldor motor. The curves use the same x and y coordinates of power in watts vs. speed in knots or mph.

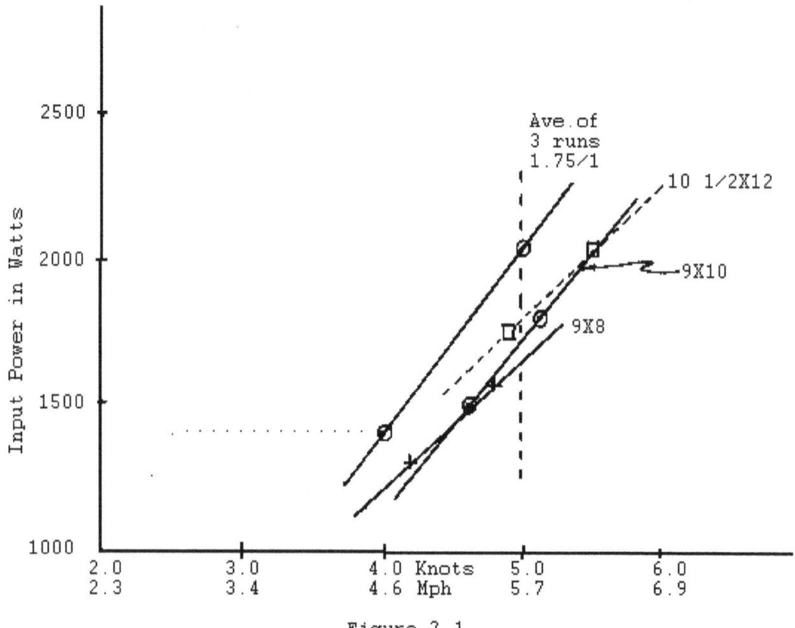

Figure 2.1
Baldor Motor in "Sunny" 2.42 to 1 Ratio vs.1.75 to 1 Ratio

The straight line labeled "Ave. of 3 runs 1.75/1" is the average of several runs with the 15 hp outboard leg with 9 x 8 and 9 x 10 propellers. The other three lines, show three different propellers that were mounted on a new 4 hp outboard leg with a 2.42 ratio.

Two boxes were constructed from this data. The first one shows a comparison between the performance of the two boats: the 20 ft O'Day and the 23 ft *Sunny*. The second box shows the effect of the reduction gear ratio of the two outboard motor legs tested on *Sunny*.

Performance Results

As Figure 2.1 shows, when the Baldor motor was mounted on an outboard motor leg with a 2.42 ratio, the performance was far better than when the same motor was mounted on a leg with a 1.75 ratio. The main reason was that the higher ratio allowed the motor to operate in a more efficient part of its power curve. A secondary reason was that the 4 hp leg had less drag than the 15 hp leg.

Comparing the 20 ft O'Day with *Sunny*

The following box shows the comparison between the two boats. Both used the same Baldor motor with the same outboard with a 1.75 ratio, but two different controllers were used for speed control. I took the average of the two best propellers at two speeds: 4 knots and 5 knots for the 20 ft O'Day (see Figure 1.1) and the average of three in-the-water runs for the 23 ft *Sunny* (see Figure 2.1). There was a substantial difference (1000 watts vs. 1400 watts) at the lower speed, but this difference was due mainly to the speed controller.

Performance Comparison between "Sunny" and 20' O'Day		
Speed in Knots	"Sunny" 1.75/1 Ratio (Watts)	20' O'Day 1.75/1 Ratio (Watts)
4.0	1064 (Corrected from 1400)	1000
5.0	2050	1800

Going back to the diagram on page 30, we notice that when running in "slow" mode, a resistor is in series with the motor. Only part of the 36 volts from the battery is dissipated by the motor; the rest is dissipated by the resistor in the form of heat and is therefore wasted. When running in "slow," the current is approximately 42 amps, causing the voltage drop across the resistor to be approximately 8 volts. Therefore, 336 watts (8 volts x 42 amps) out of the 1400 input watts never reach the motor.

In order to make an apple to apple comparison between the two boats, the slow speed of *Sunny* must be adjusted in order to compare it with the slow speed of the 20 ft O'Day (which was obtained by changing the battery taps). We must subtract 336 watts from the 1400 watts. This leaves 1064 watts, as shown in the box.

This is more in line with the 250 watt difference that we find at the higher 5 knot speed. The reason for the slightly greater input power needed to power *Sunny* is due to the larger size and heavier weight of the 23 ft boat.

Performance of "Sunny" with Two Different Ratios		
Speed in Knots	Input Power with 1.75/1 Ratio (watts)	Input Power with 2.42/1 Ratio (watts)
4.0	1400	1200
5.0	2050	1700
6.0	2500	2500(Estimate)

Improving the Efficiency with A Higher Reduction Ratio

My effort to improve the overall efficiency of the electric drive using the leg of a 4 hp Evinrude proved to be very successful. As previously mentioned it had a ratio of 2.42 to 1 rather than the 1.75 to 1 ratio of the 15 hp outboard. The higher ratio allowed the electric motor to operate at a higher rpm where its efficiency was better. I built several adapters for the propeller output shaft to test a number of different propellers. Figure 2.1 shows the results obtained from the 2.42 drive with three different propellers compared with the results of the average of several runs with the 1.75 drive.

The chart above was also constructed with data found in Figure 2.1. It clearly shows that the higher ratio is more efficient. For instance, at a speed of 5 knots, the input power is about 2050 watts for the 1.75 drive, while the average input power of the three props is only 1700 watts using the 2.42 drive. This an improvement of 17% obtained just by using the correct reduction gear ratio for this motor.

The curves also show that the two nine inch propellers perform equally well at low speed and that both are superior to the 10.5 x 12 prop. The 10.5 inch prop had too much pitch for low speed operation. The best overall performance was obtained with the 9 x 8 prop.

If the 1700 watts of input power were obtained from eight golf cart batteries generating 35 amps at 48 volts, the running time would be between five and six hours.

The End of the Season

The last thing to report on is the operation of the solar panels: they worked out very well. I used the boat once or twice a week and the solar panels kept the batteries fully charged. There was, of course, a limit to the charging power of solar panels. I found that a good rule of thumb was to allow two days of charging time for each hour of operation. In the Northeast, you can't expect sunny days every day even in the summer. And, as we will see in the theory of solar cells, the charging power drops down to a trickle when the sun hides behind the clouds.

Lessons Learned - Year Two

1. The most significant thing I found was that a 23 ft sailboat reached hull speed with a very reasonable 50 amps at 36 volts (1800 watts of input power).

2. The substantial improvement resulting from using the lower unit with the 2.42 reduction ratio versus the one with the 1.75 ratio was a pleasant and unexpected surprise.

3. A better controller than the ones I used for testing that year was needed. The main problem with the "fast/slow" controller with the series resistor was its low efficiency in the "slow" mode. A substantial amount of battery power was dissipated by the resistor and wasted in the form of heat.

Using the 24, 30 and 36 volt battery taps was a very efficient and practical way to vary the speed of the boat, but a problem occurred when the batteries needed to be charged. All batteries could not be charged at the same rate: if the charge rate was adjusted for the batteries that were used most of the time, then the ones which were underutilized got overcharged and if the rate was adjusted for the batteries used the least, then the rest were undercharged. Of course, two 6 volt chargers and one 24 volt charger could be connected in a way to custom-charge each battery individually.

4. In retrospect, I should have tried harder to find the limit of the efficiency increase as the size of the propeller was increased. As it was, the largest prop tested was a 10.5 inch propeller with an excessive 12 inch pitch for this application. Had I been able to find a 12 x 7 inch prop, I think I would have had even better results with the drive with the 2.42 ratio.

I should mention that it isn't easy to find such a prop. The problem is that most big props are designed to handle a lot of power from big engines. Consequently, the blades are much larger than needed for a 2 hp motor. The large blades cause more friction, which actually decreases the overall efficiency of the drive. The best bet might be to start with a two-bladed sailboat propeller (two-bladed props are about 2% more efficient than three-bladed props) and have the propeller reworked to shave down the blade area. We'll leave that discussion for the propeller theory section of the book.

CHAPTER 3

Sunny, Year Three

Testing and Test Equipment

Before describing the changes and the tests performed in year three, this is an appropriate time to discuss the test equipment (which you will probably not find in your toolbox) needed to perform some of these tests. If your boat was born as an electric boat, you won't do much testing, but if it was converted to electric power these tests should prove useful.

Measuring RPM's

To measure motor rpm's, I used a Stewart-Warner hand-held tachometer. It reads in both directions of rotation and can be used on flat end shafts as well as the more common shaft with a center hole. I have been very satisfied with mine. It cost about $50.00 at W.W. Grainger (a nationwide source of commercial supplies). Electronic tachometers are also available but they cost four times as much.

Measuring Force

To measure the pull generated by the electric motor in static thrust tests, I bought a 50lb brass fish scale from one of the discount boating supply houses. It cost about $25.00. I used the same fish scale for dynamometer tests. To measure pulls of 50 to 100 lbs, I used a simple pulley arrangement with a purchase of 2 to 1.

Measuring Power

On the electrical side, a voltmeter and an ammeter are needed to determine the power that the motor consumes. A digital multi-meter is the most useful. Not only does it measure the battery voltage but it also has a very accurate 50 mv. scale (a millivolt is 1000th of a volt), which is used in conjunction with a shunt.

The shunt mentioned above is used to measure current in amperes. To measure current, the ammeter must be placed in series in the circuit. That means that all of the current used to run the motor passes through the meter. Since this current can be as high as 100 amps, the meter must be very heavy duty and capable of being connected to heavy wires (probably #6 or #10). To accomplish this, a shunt, which is a calibrated resistor, is placed in the series circuit and the voltage drop across this resistor is measured.

Shunts are normally calibrated to read a standard 50 mv. at their rated value. Their rated values range from 5 to 500 amps. I like the 50 amp size because it provides a direct reading when it is connected to a multi-meter having a full scale reading of 50 mv. In other words, a reading of 15 mv. represents a current of 15 amps. Shunts can be obtained from mail order electronic distributors such as Newark Electronics for approximately $30.00.

Measuring Boat Speed

The last and most difficult measurement to obtain accurately and consistently is the speed of the boat in knots or in miles per hour (1 knot equals 1.15 mph). There are three types of knot-meters worth mentioning.

The permanently installed sailboat knot-meter typically reads from 0 to 10 knots. It has a little wheel with an attached magnet, which rotates as the boat moves. The magnet sends electrical pulses to activate the meter. The two main problems are: the meter has to be calibrated for that particular boat and the little wheel has to be kept clean and free to rotate. This type of knot-meter is the most convenient to use.

I have not had much luck with a GPS (Global Position System) to measure speed. I have used several different ones and have never obtained consistent results at low speeds. The readings jump around too much to feel confident that the reading is accurate. Top-of-the-line models rather than my hand-held model may do a better job. Unlike the in-the-water knot-meters, the GPS gives a speed based on the over-the-ground distance, causing a substantial difference in the readings going with or against the current.

Even when I had a boat knot-meter, I used the Knotstick to double check the readings. The Knotstick is a simple device that determines the speed of the boat by measuring the drag of a small plastic disk which is pulled in the water at the end of a 20 foot string. The drag of the disk acts against a calibrated spring. Three disks are provided so that the speed can be read on a 0 to 3 knot scale, a 0 to 6 scale and a 0 to 9 scale. I used this device for all the speed data and also to calibrate the boat knot-meter to make sure that all knot-meter readings were consistent. When using the Knotstick, watch out for floating seaweeds; they cause an erroneous reading by adding drag to the line. The Knotstick costs about $35.00.

To make sure that the Knotstick's readings were correct, I made numerous runs on different measured courses. Sometimes small errors (5 to 10%) occurred due to the wind or the current. I've noticed that on a very windy day, the results were always a little bit less favorable than on a day with little wind. Of course, two runs should always be made, one with the wind and one against, but it seems that what you lose going against the wind you never make up going with the wind. It probably has to do with the chop that the wind raises. The chop slows the boat going into the waves but it doesn't increase the speed going with the waves.

The Effect of the Current

The effect of the current can easily be canceled out by taking two runs: one with the current and one against. Still, you must be careful not to run in too strong a current. Consider this hypothetical case: suppose that you have laid out a 1 nautical mile course on a river. With no wind and no current, (you should be so lucky!) at a speed of 6 knots, it will take exactly 10 minutes to run the course in each direction. Later, the tide comes in and the current is exactly 1 knot. The speed being 5 knots against the current and 7 knots with the current, you now clock the time at 12 minutes and 8.6 minutes. Averaging these two numbers, you get a time of 10.3 minutes, which, in turn, yields a speed of 5.8 knots (instead of 6 knots). Not exactly right, but acceptable.

But now consider the situation where the current increases to 3 knots. The boat speed will be 3 knots against the current and 9 knots with the current. The times are now 20 minutes and 6.6 minutes, and the average becomes 13.3 minutes. Dividing 13.3 into 60 yields a speed of 4.5 knots instead of 6 knots. Obviously, the speed can't be determined by simply averaging the time of the two runs. To solve this problem, the old algebra book has to be opened to the section on simultaneous equations.

To obtain reliable results with timed runs on a measured course, pick a good day: not too much wind and not more than a 1 knot of current. This will hold the times with and against the current within 10 to 20% of each other for good average results.

Keeping Good Records

Needless to say good records must be kept. The most important thing to record is the date. Also needed for future reference is the equipment under test and the test equipment that is used. I keep everything, including the original notes made during the tests, which I later transcribe to an engineering notebook. Often, a question arises that can only be put to rest with the original data.

While reviewing some of this original data, I ran into a data sheet that had been splashed with water. In the middle there was a large brown smudge. The smudge had been circled with a neat arrow labeled "Blood." One of those rough days for in-the-water testing.

Modifications to *Sunny* for Year Three

Photo 3.1 4 HP
Outboard Leg

To get ready for the year three of testing, I made

several changes to *Sunny* over the winter. The most important was the decision to use a smaller motor. Since I had found that *Sunny* required less than 2000 watts of input power to operate at hull speed, it seemed reasonable to look for a 2 hp motor with about 2000 watts of input power that would operate at nearly full power and highest efficiency. The one that I found was an Advance DC Motor, 24 volt, 5.5 inch in diameter, weighing 28 lbs. The light weight was advantageous because the complete electric outboard weighed only 42 lbs as opposed to 85 lbs for my first electric outboard. I used the same 4 hp outboard leg with the 2.42 ratio. A 1/4 inch aluminum plate was welded to the top part of the leg to repair damage previously done during in-the-water testing. (See Photo 3.1.)

Changing to a 24 Volt System

Changing to a 24 volt system from the 36 volt system was a mixed bag of advantages and disadvantages. The good part was that I only needed to buy four batteries to replace the original six that were overdue for replacement. However, I had to replace the wiring to carry the additional current. I replaced the #10 wiring with #6 wires to carry the 60+ amps with a minimum of power loss.

The Solar Panels

The solar panels also had to be reworked for 24 volts rather than 36 volts. While I was reworking them, I solved a sticky problem concerning the location of the 36 volt panels and improved the output power at the same time.

The location problem of the 36 volt panels was that they were centered in the middle of the roof, right under the boom. The boom cast a shadow on the panels for most of the daylight hours. As we will see when we discuss solar panels, when the panels are in series, **a shadow on any one cell reduces the output of all three panels.** To avoid this problem, I was forced to take the boom down after each use.

Photo 3.2 "Sunny with the 24 Volt Solar Panels

To generate a 24 volt charging current, only two panels were needed. However, to increase the amount of charging current, I located two sets of two panels near the edge of the roof, leaving the middle open. With this location, the shadow from the boom never reached the solar panels. Then by connecting the two sets of panels in parallel, the charging current was effectively doubled. Finally, to improve the look of the roof a little bit, I added curved end panels. The finished product can be seen in Photo 3.2.

The New Controller

I bought a new solid state electronic controller to go with the new motor. I decided on the Curtis Controller, which cost about $250.00. This controller is rated at 200 amps and operates on the PWM principle. PWM stands for pulse width modulation. It means that the DC current from the battery is divided (chopped) into thousands of pulses (about 15000 pulses per second, beyond human hearing frequency). The width of each pulse is controlled. To operate at full power, the pulses are made wide enough to touch one another but for reduced speed, the pulses are reduced in width (modulated). The width of the pulses is controlled by an adjustable potentiometer (like the volume control of a radio) to provide speed control.

Photo 3.3 The New Console

To the motor this reduction in pulse width has the effect of reducing the battery voltage. The advantage of reducing the battery voltage electronically is that, unlike using a resistor, it is nearly 100% efficient.

Photo 3.3 shows the new console in which all the circuitry is housed. Located on the left are a voltmeter and an ammeter that monitor the operation of the solar panels. The ammeter that monitors the current to the motor is located on the right side of the console.

Performance Results In-the-Water Tests

The performance of the new motor was, unfortunately, nothing to brag about. Figure 3.1, which is a graph of input power vs. the boat speed, shows that up to 4.0 knots (about 4.6 mph), the speed obtained with the 24 volt motor, is very close to the speed obtained with the golf cart motor. After that point, as the input power is increased, the 24 volt motor really began to lag. At 5 knots for example, the new Advance DC motor required about 2400 watts of input power whereas the Baldor only required about 1800 watts.

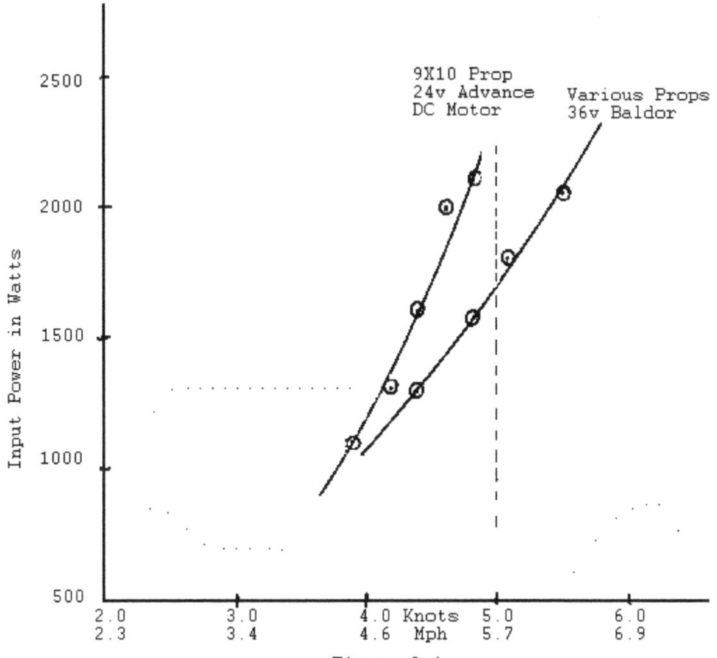

Figure 3.1
"Sunny": the Advance DC at 24v. vs. the Baldor at 36v.

Back to the Laboratory

Back in my basement laboratory, I ran dynamometer tests on the two motors. A dynamometer is a device used to measure the output power of a motor as described in Chapter 15. The results of these tests are shown in Figure 3.2. The curves show the efficiency in percent on the y axis (vertical axis) and the input power on the x axis (horizontal axis).

The results indicate two things: first, the Baldor is more efficient than the Advanced DC motor at all power levels, and second, the Baldor improves its efficiency faster as the power increases. This is consistent with the well known fact that series motors are most efficient at maximum power. It is also consistent with the fact that large motors, with their larger diameter armatures, are by nature more efficient than smaller motors.

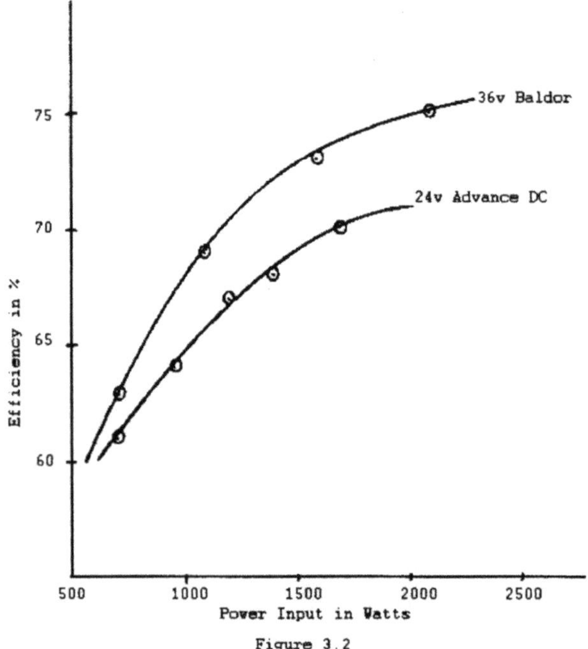

Figure 3.2
Efficiency Tests: 36v Baldor vs.24v Advance DC

After doing many dynamometer tests, I found that, of all the motors tested, the Baldor, my original golf cart motor, was, by a very small margin, the most efficient of all the DC motors that I tested. Beginner's luck, I guess.

The Dynamometer

Yes, by this time, I had built a dynamometer testing facility in my basement. With it, I could test various motors to determine their hp output and, more importantly, their efficiency. After this time, I did little in-the-water testing because the dynamometer testing was a far more accurate method to compare the characteristics of different motors. It removed all the uncertainties caused by the elements, but it was not nearly as much fun.

The Solar Panels

The performance of the solar panels was outstanding: the batteries were always charged and ready to go. And they kept up with the demand for electric power without difficulty. The only repair needed was to reseal the connections between solar panels, the instruments and the batteries. It was surprising to see how quickly the salt air attacked any exposed wire or connector and caused them to disintegrate.

Lessons Learned in Year Three

1. Special types of test equipment and good, calibrated instruments are needed to perform in-the-water tests. Keeping good records is equally important.

2. The smaller 24 volt motor mounted on the same 4 hp outboard leg with the 2.42 ratio and run with the same propellers produced disappointing results. The results were confirmed by dynamometer tests comparing the 24 volt motor with the larger Baldor.

3. After optimizing, within the limits of practicality, the shape of the boat's hull, the reduction ratio and the propeller, the efficiency of the motor became a major factor for the improvement of the electric boat's performance. This is the subject of Part 2 "Electric Boat Theory and Testing" of this book.

CHAPTER 4

Sunny, Year Four

An Inboard for *Sunny*

In the early spring of 1997, my fourth year of trying to improve the performance of the electric drive, I hoped to make two events come together. As we will see in Chapter 9, I had been making good progress on the development of a 3 phase AC motor custom designed for boat propulsion. I wanted to compare its performance with that of the DC motors that I had tested, and I also wanted to make the drive easy to modify for the testing of various propellers and drive ratios. Moreover, I wanted to improve *Sunny's* maneuverability. With the outboard motor located aft of the rudder, maneuvering in tight spaces left something to be desired.

Figure 4.1 "Sunny" as an Inboard. Outside Construction

Putting this wish list together called for *Sunny's* transformation into an inboard. The prop would be moved forward of the rudder for better maneuverability and with a belt drive, the reduction ratio would be easy to modify by changing the size of the pulleys.

I go into more construction details concerning the building of an inboard drive in Chapter 14, but at this point, I'll highlight the important steps. The skeg was cut back to make room for the propeller and a stainless steel bar was attached to the bottom to provide a pivot point for the rudder. Photo 4.1 shows the outside construction details. The skeg was then cut at an angle to accommodate a 2 inch fiberglass tube. A 2.5 inch hole was the cut out of the bottom of the hull. The tube was then fiberglassed to the hull and to the skeg. A 1.5 inch cutless bearing was slipped into the tube and locked in place with set screws at the end of the fiberglass tube. The shaft and the propeller were then installed and the rudder was replaced in its original location. With the prop directly in front of the rudder, the prop wash would now hit the rudder directly and provide excellent steerage.

Photo 4.2 "Sunny" as an Inboard: Interior construction

On the inside of the boat, shown in Photo 4.2, we see on the left a black hose that slips over the outside of the fiberglass stern tube and holds the stuffing box in place. The items mentioned, namely the stern tubing, the bearing, the hose and the stuffing box, cost about $175.00 and can be obtained at a good marine supply store. The shaft is worth shopping for because it is expensive: at least $250 including the machine work.

I used a 1 inch shaft although 7/8 of an inch would surely have done the job. But the bearing and the stuffing box for a 7/8 inch shaft were not as readily available. I believe that a bronze shaft is less expensive than a stainless steel shaft although it may not be as readily available either.

In addition to the machine work for the prop, a keyway must be machined at the spot where the drive pulley will be located. (Measure twice: machine work is expensive.) On the other side of the pulley is a pillow block type bearing, which holds up the end of the shaft. The picture shows the 1/2 inch blocks of aluminum that I used for the base of the pillow block. I might have overdone it a bit, but the pillow block did need a solid base because it transmits the push from the propeller (the axial force) to the hull of the boat.

The motor was mounted on a slide arrangement to properly tension the V belt. The arrangement shown in the picture did not work well. A belt tensioner such as a spring loaded idler pulley that presses against the belt was needed to prevent the belt from slipping at full power.

Performance Results

In its third year, *Sunny* didn't get into the water until after the Fourth of July due to the extensive modifications. My friends accuse me of doing more “backyard boating” than in-the-water boating. That turned out to be true these last two years. But it was worth it. The inboard performed beautifully. Especially noteworthy was the maneuverability that the inboard provided. It didn't quite make a U turn in its own length, but it was close. The only problem was that, at full power, the belt tended to slip unless it was perfectly adjusted. The solar panels continued to keep the batteries fully charged for each outing.

The only in-the-water test results I recorded that year were the full power speed of 4.5 knots at 65 amps (1560 watts) and the 4 knot speed at 50 amps (1200 watts). A comparison of the results from the inboard and the outboard versions of *Sunny* are shown in Figure 4.1 below.

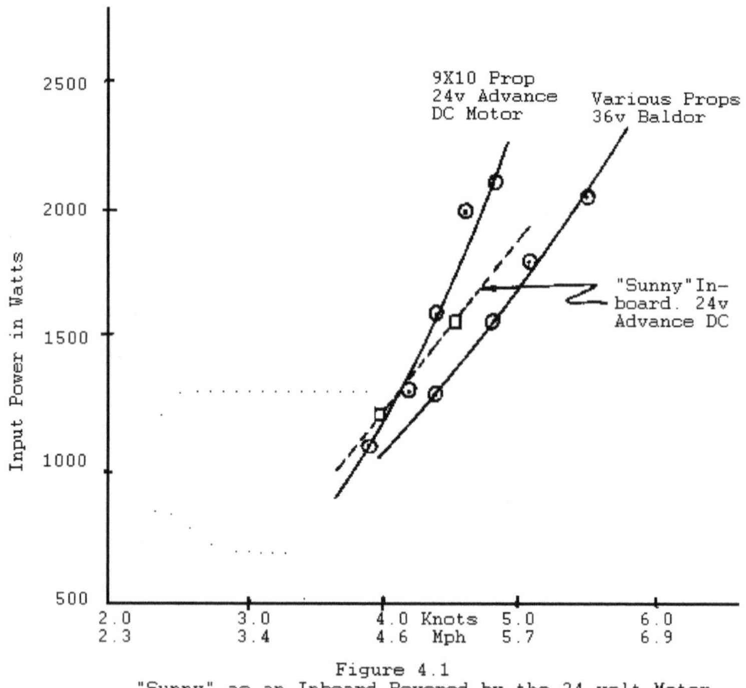

Figure 4.1
"Sunny" as an Inboard Powered by the 24 volt Motor

Figure 4.1 shows that in either configuration, inboard or outboard, the 24 volt motor provides approximately the same speed. It also shows that this speed is substantially less than the results obtained with the Baldor 36 volt motor. I tried various motor pulleys to increase the ratio, but that effort did not yield any noticeable improvement.

The End of Another Season

After Labor Day, as I was struggling to take my 200 lb mooring out of the East Bay muck, I spotted a marina operator who was installing winter stakes on some of his year-round moorings. Moorings have to be pulled and inspected every three years in the town of Barnstable. He told me that for $25.00 he would bring my mooring to his yard and help me load it on my trailer. A bargain, believe me. Meanwhile, his two associates, who were guarding the pickup truck while he was doing all the work, asked me if I wanted to sell my mooring. We agreed on $100 "as is, where is" and that was the end of some twenty five years of boating around East Bay, one of the prettiest spots on Cape Cod. (see photo 4.3 below)

Photo 4.3 "Sunny", Erin, Big Charlie and Daniel

On my way home, contemplating what I had just done, I decided to buy a boat that I could trailer easily and do my boating a little closer to home. *Sunny* weighed over 3000 lbs, which is a handful to trailer and launch. I figured that a motorboat in the 1500 lb range might be a nice change. So, I did what boaters like to do best: plan for the new boat. I knew that I would be boating mostly in Boston Harbor, not offshore, so I thought that a well appointed Carolina Skiff would do the trick. For power, I thought that one of the new 4 cycle outboards would be an interesting motor to try out. And, of course, I would install a bracket on the transom to mount an electric kicker. By the time I arrived home, I felt a lot better.

Lessons Learned

1. My program to test the effects of larger propellers, various reduction ratios and, possibly, a 3 phase AC motor proved to be too ambitious and did not produce any substantial results. I did find out that the inboard power worked out very well: steering and maneuverability being particularly good. The 3 phase AC work progressed too slowly to be tested in the inboard configuration of *Sunny*.

I found that by simulating the motor tests on a dynamometer, the results of the in-the-water tests were emphasized. This was clearly shown in Figure 3.2: the performance of the Baldor vs. the Advance DC Motor. I have no doubt that dynamometer tests of the 3 phase AC motor will be equally enlightening without the need of extensive in-the-water testing.

2. The main problem with the inboard was the slipping belt. And the main reason that I could not fix it in the water was that I had not provided sufficient access to the mechanism. It was tricky to work on the motor when the boat was securely on its trailer, but to attempt to do this work while the boat was bouncing around in the water was just too difficult. My first task should have been to install a large access hatch in the floor even if it meant ruining the looks of the floor with the new mahogany strips.

3. In its inboard configuration, *Sunny* was a most pleasant boat in which to spend an afternoon with the grandkids. I'll miss her. (See Photo 4.3.) I donated *Sunny* to a maritime school; hopefully, some budding engineer will find electric propulsion for boats a worthwhile challenge.

CHAPTER 5

The Carolina Skiff, Year Five

The New Carolina Skiff

I seldom buy a new boat: they are too expensive and depreciate too fast for my boating budget. However, the Carolina Skiff is quite inexpensive and can be bought as a basic hull or with a whole list of add-ons. I went half way with the factory installed decks, railings, and a console with the steering and the motor controls installed. (The end of the season special price for the 21 ft model was a bit under $7000.00.)

The main reason for choosing the Carolina Skiff was its renowned low resistance hull. I figured it would be easy to plane with a relatively small primary power outboard (50 to 80 hp) and it would operate easily at hull speed with an electric kicker. The hull was built like a huge ice cube tray with a flat bottom and wide bow. It was not a beautiful boat: the interior was not finished. It was designed more as a work boat or a fishing boat. And it was not a boat that you would want to take offshore in any kind of surf. The flat bottom gave a very rough ride. But the boat was rugged, inexpensive and easy on the gas.

The Power Plant

When it came to buying the outboard, I was very much tempted to go with the Honda 4 cycle 50 hp motor, but the $4000.00+ price tag frightened me. Also, I was concerned that the boat would be underpowered with that engine. The next larger size, the 80 hp Honda was nearly twice as expensive and weighed over 400 lbs, which was way out of my price and strength range.

Instead, I found an old 50 hp Evinrude that was ideal to test out the boat and to determine the best motor size. I found that although the boat did indeed plane with the 50 hp motor, it felt underpowered with more than two people on board. I kept the outboard one season and found a very nice second-hand 70 hp Evinrude, which was just right for the boat: it got on a plane quickly and flew at 32 mph. I sold the 50 hp for what I paid for it. (It never fails to amaze me how easy it is to buy and sell used outboard motors.)

A Few Additions for Creature Comfort

I made a few additions to the boat: a large bimini and a porta-potty under the rear deck. From the bimini, I hung a privacy curtain that looked a little like a shower stall. Nothing fancy but the grandkids (who always need to go when they go boating) liked it. See Photo 5.4 of the whole gang at the end of this chapter.

Console Modifications

With the flat floor, there was not too much choice for the location of the batteries. I didn't want to add any more weight to the stern, so that left only the console. Fortunately, there was just enough room for four #27, 12 volt deep cycle batteries. (See Photo 5.1.) I cut an opening in the front of the console and installed a large hatch to provide access to the batteries.

Photo 5.2 shows the modified console. The electronic controller and the control switches (bottom row of switches and the digital ammeter) all fit neatly inside the console. The rest of the electrical equipment for the outboard motor was installed under the rear deck.

Photo 5.1 The Battery Box Built in the Console

Photo 5.2 C.S. Console with the Added Switches and Meter

The New Electric Power Plant

I built a new electric outboard for the Skiff based on a 5 hp Johnson outboard leg. It had a reduction ratio of 2.08 to 1. Not quite as good as the 4 hp's 2.42 to 1 ratio but the best that I could find. There were very few older outboard motors on the market with a higher ratio.

Photo 5.3 5HP Leg with 48v. Motor

The main reason for going for the 5 hp leg was that the 4 hp leg was not quite rugged enough for my new 47 lb GE 3 hp electric motor (20 lbs heavier than the Advance DC 2 hp motor). The mounting bracket, in particular, was a little flimsy for a heavy electric motor. An interesting feature of the 4 hp was that, unlike any other outboard that I've seen, it had a left-hand prop. As far as the electric motor was concerned, it was only necessary to operate the motor in a counter-clockwise, instead of a clockwise direction, when a right hand prop was used (left hand props are rarely found on the used market). I did notice that the reduction gears were noisier when the motor was made to rotate in the opposite direction.

Photo 5.3 shows the finished 5 hp leg with the 48 volt GE motor. The mounting plate for the electric motor was made of 1/4 inch aluminum plate. The rest is straightforward except for the 3 inch plug between the two lower sections of the leg. This was the place where a 5 inch plug would be inserted if it were a “long shaft” (20 inch shaft) motor rather than a “short shaft” (15 inch shaft) motor.

The reason for the 3 inch plug was to accommodate the spline coupler that I built (more about couplers in Chapter 13). It fits on the drive shaft of the outboard on one end and on the shaft of the electric motor on the other end. This extra length worked well when the motor was mounted on an outboard bracket.

The propeller shaft was modified to accommodate the 9 x 10 inch prop that was used in many previous tests with many other motors.

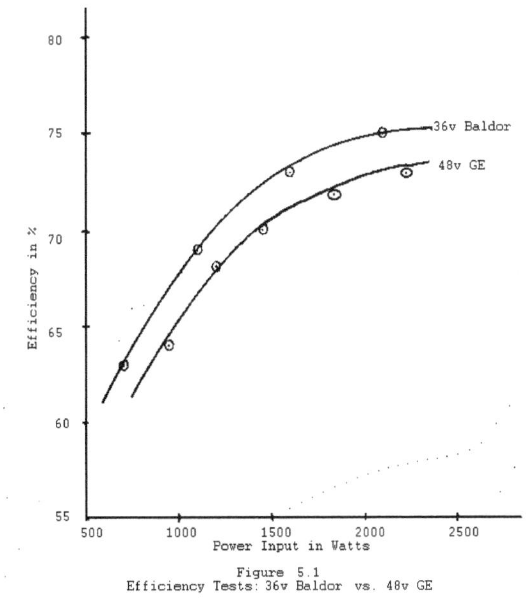

Figure 5.1
Efficiency Tests: 36v Baldor vs. 48v GE

The new electric motor was a 48 volt GE replacement motor that I bought from Mort Ray. As we will see later in the book, Mort and I collaborated on some electric motor efficiency tests. By using one of his motors, I was able to get performance data to compare it with other DC motors as well as the 3 phase AC motor that I was developing at the time.

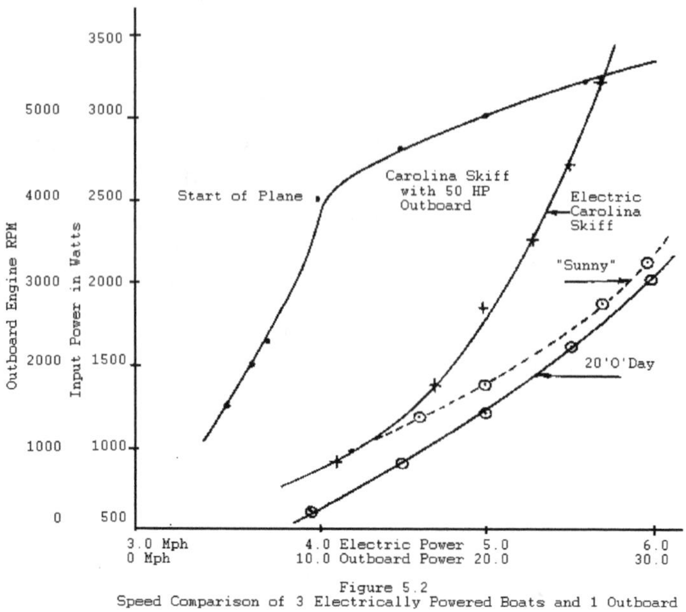

Figure 5.2
Speed Comparison of 3 Electrically Powered Boats and 1 Outboard

The GE motor weighed 47 lbs and the entire electric outboard weighed 64 lbs. The efficiency of the motor is shown in Figure 5.1. This figure also shows the efficiency curves of the Baldor golf cart motor for comparison. As we can see, the two motors are nearly equal in performance with a slight 2% edge going to the Baldor in this output range. At a higher power range, the efficiency of the GE improves and matches that of the Baldor. It is therefore safe to assume that the efficiency shown here (a maximum of 75%) is about as good as can be obtained with any series wound DC motor.

Performance Results
Gas Powered Outboard Performance

Figure 5.2, which has two sets of coordinates, shows the performance of the 50 hp gas outboard and of the new electric outboard motor. The curve for the 50 hp outboard is a plot of the speed (in RPMs) of the motor against the speed of the boat (in mph) on the lower line of speed numbers. At 1600 rpm, the boat moves at 5 mph. It starts to plane at 10 mph as the motor revs up to 4000 rpm. After that point, the speed increases very rapidly to 26 mph at 5200 rpm.

Electric Power Performance of the Carolina Skiff

With the electric outboard (using the other set of coordinates), the curve shows that the boat will not exceed hull speed (about 5 mph) without requiring a great deal of additional power. This is another "bottom line" curve of power in watts vs. boat speed. Notice that about 2000 watts is required to reach 5 mph, but to go 1/2 mph faster requires about 3000 watts.

Carolina Skiff's Performance Compared with the Sailboat's

The Carolina Skiff was much lighter than the sailboats (1500 lbs vs. 3000 lbs for *Sunny*), yet it required much more power than the sailboats. For instance, starting at 5 mph, the 20 ft O'Day took 1200 watts, *Sunny* took 1350 watts and the Skiff required 1800 watts. At 5.5 mph the power requirement was about 1600 watts for the sailboats and nearly twice as much for the Skiff, a difference of about 1400 watts.

The reason is that, although the hull of the Skiff had an excellent design to attain planing speed and a high cruising speed with low power, it had a short waterline and more wetted surface than a sailboat of the same size. Hull speed was reached at a lower speed and after that point, the power requirement increased very rapidly.

Lessons Learned in Chapter 5

1. The Carolina Skiff was a fine boat for its designed purpose. It had spacious floor area with large carrying capacity as we see in Photo 5.4. It had a very rugged construction and was capable of achieving high speeds with a small power plant. But, because of the shape of its hull, it did not come close to the performance of the sailboats at hull speed.

2. The 48 volt system worked very well. I used a solid state Curtis Controller for speed control. To charge the batteries, I used two 12 volt battery chargers wired in series to obtain 24 volts so that two batteries could be charged at one time. By leaving the chargers on for twenty-four hours on each pair of batteries each time I used the boat, the batteries were always fully charged.

Photo 5.4 The Whole Gang on the Carollina Skiff

CHAPTER 6

SUNNY II, a RHODES 19

The new sailboat

A full year after writing "Electric Propulsion for Boats" (2002), I decided to use all the knowledge I had gained and convert one more boat to electric power. It had to be a sailboat because the hulls of readily available motor boats are just not designed to operate at hull speed. The experiment with the Carolina skiff was ample proof of that.

I had looked for an O'Day Rhodes 19 on and off in the past but I could not find one at a reasonable price. Then one day, a boater advertised four of them for sale. He had raced the Rhodes 19 for years and had accumulated a barn full of boats and all sorts of parts and accessories. By the time I got to his house on Cape Cod, he had sold two of them and he was holding a third one for a friend. The 1970 Rhodes 19 that was left was truly in tough shape. It had been beached during a hurricane damaging the hull, the rudder was lost, some of the floor boards were broken and the centerboard was wedged in the trunk.

He did have it on a good trailer and he was selling it with an expensive tapered mast to replace the missing one. The price was commensurate with the damaged goods and I quickly snapped it up.

I spent the whole summer getting it back in presentable shape. The previous owner was very helpful: he had lots of spare parts for the Rhodes 19 such as floor boards and he had a milling machine to remove the damaged surface of the wood to bring the mahogany back to its original beauty. I built a mahogany rudder from a copy of the original and since I would be installing heavy batteries in the boat, I built a lightweight fiberglass centerboard to replace the cast iron one. Three suits of sails came with the boat. None were very good but I selected the best of the bunch and decided to make do with that. The rest of the repairs took a great deal of elbow grease but came out spectacularly well.

The only improvement that I made to the boat was to install a tabernacle which is a pivot at the bottom of the mast. Normally, the mast slips through a hole in the ceiling of the cabin and rests on the keel. Without the tabernacle, stepping the mast with the boat on a trailer is a difficult operation and it is almost impossible to do single handed.

To support the tabernacle, I used one of my slightly bent 1" propeller shaft from my drive shaft collection (see photo 6.2). It worked out very well. Since 5 of the 6 stays could remain attached and properly adjusted, stepping the mast with the tabernacle turned into a very simple operation.

I did add wheel steering (which would repulse Rhodes 19 purists) but I wanted to do my motoring in style and that worked out very well also. Before selling the boat I removed most of the modifications that I had made and found a very happy buyer: when I asked him if he liked the boat, his response was "What is there not to like?"

Sunny II Restored

Photo 6.1 on the next page, shows the restoration work performed on Sunny II. The new rudder is an exact copy of the original with many layers of mahogany glued together. The new console with the electric instruments and the steering was built up from the smallest Carolina Skiff console. With a cushion, the rear deck could be used as a seat. The picture shows the two openings for storage in the cuddy cabin. The space below was modified for the storage of the batteries. Three number 27, deep cycle batteries just fit in that space.

Photo 6.1 "Sunny II" Restored with New Rudder and Console

Battery Storage

Photo 6.2 on the next page is a close up of the storage area in the bow, where life jackets, anchor and other large items can be stowed. Below, I added a shelf and a large access hatch to reach the three 24 volt batteries housed there. Note the vents on each side of the hatch.

The bronze shaft is the support for the tabernacle which I installed on the cabin top for the new tapered mast.

Photo 6.2 "Sunny II" Battery Box and Tabernacle Support

Sunny II's Inboard

Photo 6.3 "Sunny II" Inboard Construction with Etek Motor

The construction of Sunny II's inboard was considerably simpler than Sunny's. By eliminating the reduction gear, the Etek motor which has a 7/8 inch drive shaft could be connected directly with a Lovejoy coupler (shown) or a solid coupler to the propeller shaft which was also 7/8 inch in diameter.

Looking at Photo 6.3, we see at the far left the 1 ¾ inch fiberglass stern tube (outside diameter) which was fiberglassed in the bottom of the boat at an angle of approximately 15 degrees to the water line.

The black hose which is 4 ½ inches long with an inside diameter of 1¾ was attached to the stern tube with the other end connected to the 1¾ inch body of the stuffing box. The collar on the shaft was installed to stop the shaft from pulling out of the coupler. With a solid coupler which I used for most of the in-the-water testing, this is unlikely to happen. But, remember that if the prop and shaft should slide out of the boat, they would be lost and the boat would be left with a one inch opening to the water.

The stainless steel shaft is 7/8 inch in diameter and 48 inches long. I bought it as replacement shaft from "Boat US" (now West Marine) for $250 with all the standard machine work already done. The shaft was attached to the coupler and then to the Etek drive motor.

Under the boat, photo 6.4 shows the strut holding up the other end of the shaft as well as the reworked propeller. The strut angle is not adjustable but its 20 degree angle and the 6 ½ inch dimension from the base of the strut to the center of the shaft provides the exact angle needed to keep the shaft angle at a minimum. The best possible drive efficiency is obtained with a low shaft angle.

A cutless bearing was inserted in the bottom part of the strut. It has the same inside diameter as the propeller shaft and of the same length as the strut. Cutless bearings are made of ribbed rubber allowing water to circulate in the grooves and lubricate the bearing surface. With proper alignment, they require no adjustment and last for many years.

The stuffing box mentioned above is designed to seal the rotating shaft so that sea water will not enter the boat. A packing nut with a locking nut squeezes the packing material (cotton rope impregnated with graphite) just enough to allow the shaft to turn freely but stop the water from flowing in. The rule is to have no leaking when the shaft is stopped and one drop per minute when the shaft turns. If you are lucky enough to achieve this goal lock the setting in place…post haste!

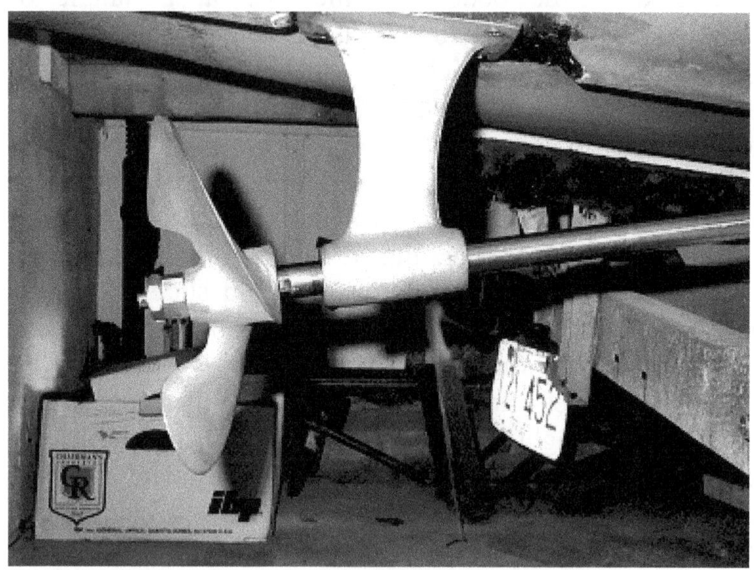

Photo 6.4 "Sunny II" Outside Construction

The alignment of the strut and the motor shaft are key to a quiet, vibration free and efficient operation. The stuffing box, being attached to a rubber hose will adjust slightly to the alignment of the shaft. However, with the walls of the hose fully 5/16 inch thick and the hose being quite short, there is very little give: it needs to be centered and aligned along with the other components.

While doing some alignment work on the shaft, I discovered a fool proof way to determine the best possible shaft alignment. When all the components are properly positioned, the motor should be adjusted in height and angle so that a solid coupler, 7/8 inch in diameter can slide from the driveshaft onto the motor shaft without undue strain. The final, fine adjustments can then be done electrically. The no load current to the motor with a 12 volt source is measured with the shaft disconnected. Say it measures 4 amps. The shaft is then connected and the current is measured a second time, (after lubricating the cutless bearing and the stuffing box with a shot of WD-40). If the current does not increase by more than 1 amp, the alignment is acceptable provided that the motor mounting bolts are tightened to their final torque setting.

More construction details are provided in Part 3 the "Build it Yourself Projects" section of this book. The alignment procedure described above was duplicated on the bench so that the shim sizes needed to obtain the correct alignment could be correlated with the electric measurements.

Why an O'Day Rhodes 19?

Besides saying that I always liked the looks of the Rhodes 19 and wanted to own one, it was just the right size for me. Not too big to trailer, yet roomy enough for 5 or 6 people. As a candidate for an electric drive, it had a fairly wide beam (7 feet) but it was fairly light: with the lighter center board, the 3 batteries and the console it weighed about 1200 pounds.

I had promised myself to measure the amount of pull needed to drag it in the water at hull speed before buying my next boat, but I never did. I reasoned that a boat with such a successful racing record must be well designed and slippery in the water. I was not disappointed.

Although I did more motoring than sailing, it was a nice change of pace to take it for a sail when the wind cooperated. Hingham Harbor which is within Boston Harbor is the home of a small fleet of Rhodes 19's.

The New Etek Motor

When I surveyed all the possible motors that were suitable for electric propulsion of boats, I was very impressed by the Lynch motor developed in the UK specifically for boat propulsion. The motor is light in weight, the speed is low at low battery voltages and, due to permanent magnet field, its efficiency is very high.

Except for the price which was three times as much as other DC motors of its size, it was the perfect boat motor.

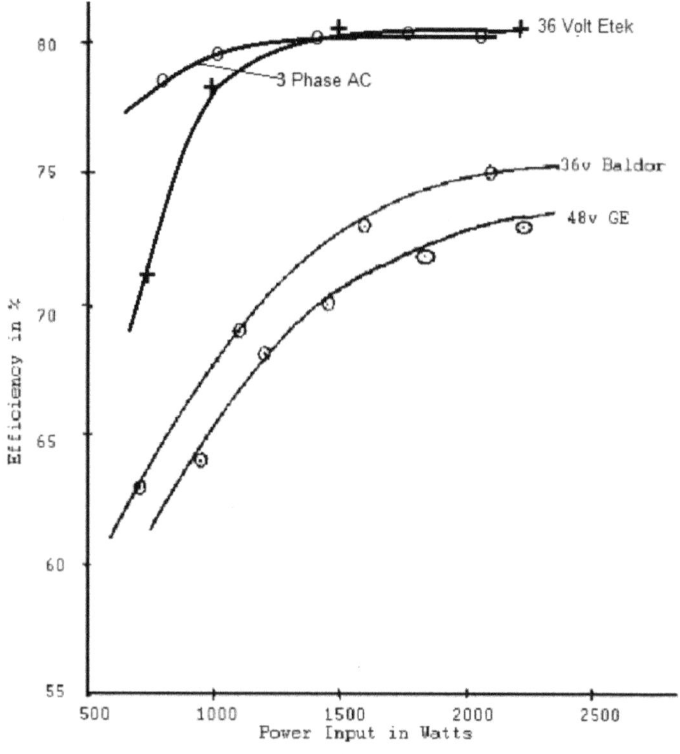

Figure 6.1 Efficiency of the Etek Motor

Mainly because of the high price of specialty motors

like the Lynch motor, I carried on a research and development program hoping to find other efficient electric boat motors. I concentrated on the 3 phase AC motor which could run on DC batteries with an appropriate inverter/controller and would have equally good efficiency. It would also be safer for boating applications because it had no commutator and it had the potential of being even less expensive than the "golf cart" DC motors that were available at the time. The 3 phase AC motor will be discussed in Part 2.

Around that time (2002), Briggs and Stratton bought a license to build and sell the Lynch motor under the name Etek. The motor was built in China. It sold for a price competitive with other DC motors of that horsepower: about $400. Today, the Etek R is available for about $470.

Figure 6.1 (above) shows the dynamometer test results on 3 DC motors suitable for powering a boat like the Rhodes 19. The impressive Etek is nearly 10% more efficient than my original golf cart Baldor or the GE motor that was used in the Ray electric outboards at that time. Notice also that, unlike the other two DC motors, the efficiency remains high even though the motor operates at less than full power.

Figure 6.1 also compares the Etek motor with the 3 phase AC motor which was used in the "big test" at Mort Ray's shop. The efficiencies are very comparable but notice that the 3 Phase AC motor's efficiency remains even higher at very low power requirements. This AC motor was a prototype and every indication pointed to higher efficiencies as the motor continued to be refined with better Mosfet switches in the inverter/controller.

My dynamometer results on the Etek motor were about 5% less than the published results as they were for all the other motors that I tested. This is due mostly to the power lost in the bearings of the dynamometer as well as some wind losses that don't show up in the pull of the spring scale readings.

In the Water Test Results

The in-the-water tests results (as seen in figure 6.2) compare the results of the other two sailboats tested with the Rhodes 19. Readings obtained from the curves show that it takes far less power to drive the Rhodes than the other boats. For example, at 5 mph the Rhodes requires 500 watts while the other 2 boats average about 1200 watts. At 6 mph, the Rhodes requires 1000 watts while the other two boats need 2000 watts.

At 19' 2" the Rhodes is the smallest of the 3 boats and the lightest. It weighs about 1200 lbs compared to the O'Day 20 at 2000 lbs and the 23 foot Sunny at 3000 lbs. Nevertheless, these very low power requirements are impressive and are due in large measure to the efficiency of the Etek motor.

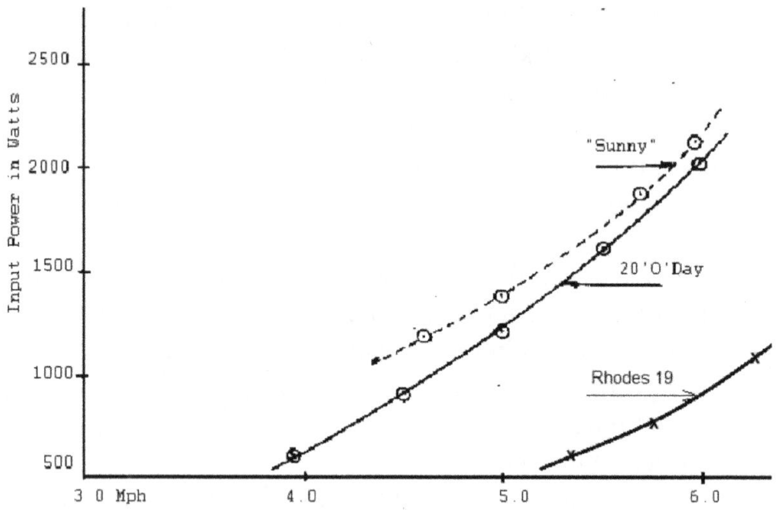

Figure 6.2 Input Power of Rhodes 19 vs. two Sailboats

In the box below, I added a column to a previously shown box to compare the Rhodes 19 results with those of the 20' O'Day and the 23 foot "Sunny".

Performance Comparison between "Sunny", 20' O'Day, and the Rhodes 19			
Speed in Knots	"Sunny" 1.75/1 Ratio (Watts)	20' O'Day 1.75/1 Ratio (Watts)	Rhodes 19 9X6 Prop (Watts)
4.0	1064 (Corrected from 1400)	1000	400
5.0	2050	1800	750

The results show that less than one half of the power is needed to move the Rhodes 19 compared to the other boats. These results are amazing but absolutely correct. We have been saying that for best results, the efficiency of the boat hull, the motor and the prop have to be optimized. This is the proof of the pudding!

With just three #27 deep cycle batteries discharging at less than 25 amps, the range for this boat is about 20 miles at 5.5 miles per hour.

Unfortunately, I do have in-the-water performance results for the 3 hp 3 phase AC motor in Sunny II. From the dynamometer tests we can tell that the efficiency of the two motors is almost equal and the low speed characteristics of 3 phase AC motors would make it even easier to match it to an efficient propeller for a direct drive. I would therefore expect exceptionally good results from a three phase AC motor also.

Propellers for the Rhodes 19

Another factor that contributed to the excellent results shown above is the choice of a proper propeller. Figure 6.3 below summarizes the results of in-the-water tests with various propellers. Four propellers were used for numerous in the water tests: A plastic 12x6, a brass 10x6, a brass 9x8 and finally the best prop, the 9x8 brass prop that was re-pitched into a 9x6 propeller.

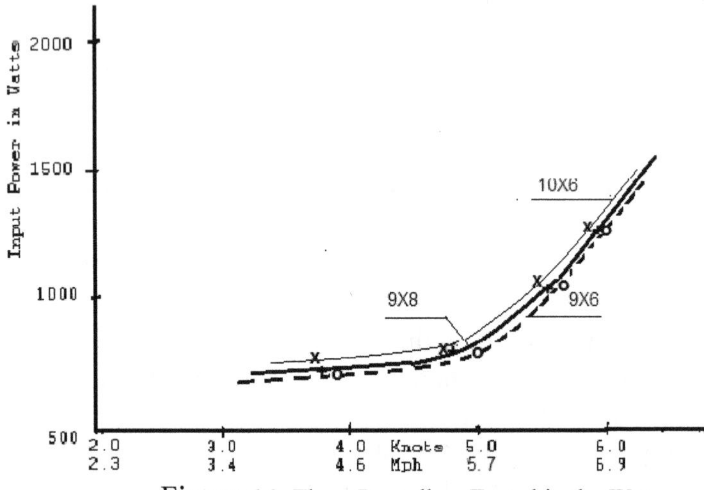

Figure 6.3 Three Propellers Tested in the Water

Early during the prop testing, I determined that the plastic 12x6 prop did not give better results than the brass 9x8 prop. It was therefore set aside while the testing of the other props proceeded.

Figure 6.3 above shows the average of many runs. The difference between props is not great, but it does show that the reworked brass 9x8 prop with the new pitch making it a 9x6 prop gives the best results.

The 9x6 propeller curve was used in figure 6.2 to compare the performance of the Rhodes 19 with the performance of the other two sailboats.

Drive shaft Alignment

An important consideration when attempting to obtain maximum efficiency is not to waste power in the shaft bearings. Misaligned bearings cause unwanted noise and vibrations.

As I mentioned before, with an electric drive, the fine adjustments for a perfect alignment can be made electrically. I set up a drive shaft mockup on a work bench complete with strut, stuffing box and Etek motor to simulate the full drive train that was used in Sunny II. My hope was to obtain a good correlation between out of line situations and the extra amount of current required. More about shaft alignment in Chapter 14.

Lessons Learned in Part 1- First 6 Chapters

In the first six chapters, we saw some very good examples of substantial improvements in performance in two of the three major areas of concern, namely:

The hull, where the sailboat hulls were so much more efficient at hull speed than the hull of the Carolina Skiff.

The correct propeller speed. We found that the electric outboard with a 2.42 reduction ratio provided a measurable improvement over the 1.75 ratio when used with a properly sized propeller.

We found that when the more efficient Baldor motor was replaced with the smaller Advance DC motor, the performance suffered badly. Part 2 of the book is dedicated to solving this third area of concern, namely what can be done to improve the efficiency of the electric motor.

We also found that an electric boat conversion based on a very efficient hull and a very efficient Etek motor installed as an inboard propulsion system provided unbeatable results. Equally good results would result from the use of a 3 Phase AC motor.

Part 2 of the book "Electric Boat Theory and Testing" includes two chapters on the specifications of a number of different DC motors. These are compared to a 3 phase AC motor which, with its custom designed controller, operates on DC batteries. Dynamometer tests are run to compare the performance of these motors.

Four more chapters are dedicated to the theory of electric motors, boat hulls, propellers, and batteries.

PART 2

Electric Boat Theory And Testing

CHAPTER 7

Survey of DC Motors

In the first six chapters, four boats were converted to run on battery power with four different electric motors. The main purpose was to determine which configuration would perform best. Best performance means obtaining the highest possible speed and the longest range with the least amount of power drain from the battery.

Recapping what we learned from the boat conversions: we determined that sailboat hulls have less resistance than motorboat hulls and therefore perform better. Although we did not attempt to find the ultimate low resistance hull because it would not be practical for all-around pleasure boating, we did find that 1500 to 2000 watts of battery power was adequate to obtain hull speed in a well designed boat.

At 48 volts, that would mean a drain of 30 to 40 amps. At this level of battery drain, using eight golf cart batteries, a range of 30 miles at 5 mph was easily attainable (the running time would be about six hours). We continue the discussion of low resistance hulls in Chapter 10.

We tried a variety of propellers at various reduction gear ratios. The results indicated what was common knowledge: that a large slow turning prop was more efficient than a small prop spinning at high rpm, but once in the right ballpark, the difference in performance between propellers was much harder to detect.

For example, it was easy enough to see that an 8 x 7 1/4 inch prop was too small in diameter and had too little pitch, but when the results from two 9 inch props were compared, one with an 8 inch pitch and the other with a 9 inch pitch, the results were nearly identical.

The conclusion is that, considering the restrictions that a small boat presents to the use of very large propellers, a 9 to 12 inch diameter prop with the correct pitch works very well in boats 19 to 23 feet long. Of course, the pitch must be selected to match the electric motor's most efficient rpm with a given reduction ratio. More about the theory of propellers is presented in Chapter 11.

That brings us to the electric motors, which were used in the boats. Four different motors were tested. The Baldor golf cart motor, the smaller 5.5 inch diameter Advance DC motor, the GE motor, similar in size to the Baldor and the very efficient Etek motor. The Baldor and the GE gave very similar results, but the smaller motor, even though it operated at its maximum power output (where it should be most efficient) gave the worst results. There are two explanations for these results: first, larger motors in general, are more efficient than small ones; second, all motors are not designed equally well when it comes to efficiency. For example, it could be that efficiency of the smaller motor was traded off for lighter weight. The Etek motor, specifically designed originally for boating applications was far and away the best of breed.

Researching Other Motor Options

While I was doing the motor testing, I did some serious research about all off-the-shelf electric motors. With the help of the Thomas Register (or ThomasNet on line), which occupies about 6 feet of shelf space in the library and lists hundreds of companies which build all types of motors for hundreds of different applications, I made a list of twenty companies and inquired about their products.

The criteria used for the inquiries were as follows:

The operating voltage had to be 36 volts DC plus or minus 12 volts.

The horsepower had to be in the 2 to 3 hp range.

The weight had to be as light as possible and the size had to be as small as possible, but realistically, the motor probably would have a diameter of 6 to 7 inches and the weight would probably be in the 30 to 50 lb range.

Efficiency was considered very important with a goal of 80%.

The motor had to be capable of running continuously at its rated power.

Surprisingly, this extensive research yielded very few worthwhile results. Most of the motors were for automotive use and ran on 12 volts. Most of the lightweight motors could not be used for continuous duty. And, in most cases, efficiency was not an important factor for the manufacturer or was not available in the specifications. (I might also mention that more than half of the companies did not reply to my inquiries.)

Permanent Magnet Motors

At the time, I thought a motor that used permanent magnets in its field instead of the wound field would surely be more efficient. I concentrated on the companies that offered these motors. The closest I came to an acceptable motor was a replacement motor used to lift snowplows or other heavy accessories, but it ran only intermittently and on 12 volts.

I did find another company that made custom permanent magnet motors, which met the requirements listed above, but the price was out of sight. So much for the search for off-the-shelf DC motors. To this day, I have yet to hear of a DC motor made for another application (not boating) that beats the golf cart motor.

Library Research

I spent a considerable amount of time in the technical libraries of MIT and Northeastern University (my Alma Mater) and obtained a listing of some 100 books written in the last twenty years about all types of electric motors and motor controllers. Most of the books were learned dissertations filled with long formulas with little practical value as far as my boating research was concerned.

Occasionally, I did pick up a gem of an idea, particularly concerning motor efficiency. And, there were some practical books, which covered the subject thoroughly with up-to-date information. In particular, I liked Irving M. Gottlieb's "Electric Motors and Control Technique." It does a fine job covering the theory of both the AC and DC motors as well as the controllers used to start them and control their speed.

The Brushless DC Motor

After the library research, I felt that there were two types of motors worth considering in addition to the golf cart motor. One was the so-called brushless DC motor and the other was the 3 phase AC motor. The advantage of the brushless DC motor was that the commutation function normally done by the commutator and the brushes of the DC motor was done electronically. Coupled with the use of permanent magnets for its fields, this motor was very efficient. Moreover, it solved the maintenance problem that DC motors have, namely the need to replace the brushes.

Most of these motors are small (mostly fractional hp) and they are custom designed for specific applications. Not being mass-produced, the cost is three or four that of a mass-produced motor that you'd find listed in W.W. Grainger's catalog. But they certainly have a good basic design and the potential of an excellent, efficient boat motor.

The 3 Phase AC Motor

Until the advent of modern electronics, one would not even have considered the use of an AC motor for a portable application. Batteries produce DC not AC; but DC can be converted to AC without significant power loss using switching devices, which are both efficient and inexpensive. (The words "converter" and "inverter" are sometimes used interchangeably. My understanding is that "converting" is going from AC to DC and "inverting" is going from DC to AC.) So, to run an AC motor from batteries, an AC inverter is needed and, if the motor is a 3 phase motor, then a 3 phase inverter is needed.

AC Motors

As is the case with DC motors, AC motors come in an endless variety of packages, voltages, single or multiple phase, and, depending on the application, with a variety of starting devices.

The choice between single phase and 3 phase motors is easy: everything that the single phase motor can do, the 3 phase motor can do better. It is lighter, smaller and more efficient. Its speed is adjustable and it does not require additional components to produce excellent starting torque. The downside is that 3 phase inverters necessary to make them run from battery power are not as readily available as single phase inverters.

3 Phase AC Motors

Still, I opted for the 3 phase AC motor as the best candidate for powering boats. Compared to the DC motors, they are less expensive by a factor of two, they are more readily available, and, with a properly designed inverter/controller, they have all the desirable features that I was looking for in a DC motor. The 3 phase AC motors are smaller and lighter than their DC counterparts. They have adequate starting torque for boating applications and rotate at relatively low speed: 1750 rpm at 60 cycles and 1450 rpm at 50 cycles. Because they have no brushes and have only one moving part, they are the safest, most reliable and maintenance-free motor available. In addition, they have the potential of being substantially more efficient.

Designed for Efficient Operation

As the workhorse of industry, 3 phase AC motors are manufactured by the millions by at least thirty different manufacturers. This type of competition insures a low price and constantly improving quality, particularly in terms of efficiency. Not only do the competitive brands attempt to design the most efficient motor possible, but governments of many nations, recognizing that these motors use a substantial percentage of the power generated in the world, have also dictated minimum efficiency standards. As of October 1997, all 3 phase AC motors manufactured in the United States are of premium quality and adhere to a set of efficiency standards. Listed in the box below are a few motors in the hp range that we will be considering. They are all 4 pole (1800 rpm) "open" motors (enclosed motors need a fan for cooling and are about 2% less efficient).

Although the NEMA (National Electrical Manufacturer's Association) standard for efficient motors is 93% for 50 hp motors, some of the manufacturers exceed this standard. In fact, from 1975 to 1995, the average efficiency of 50 hp motors has improved from 91 to 95%.

Two interesting books on the subject are Todd Litman's *Efficient Electric Motor Systems* and John C. Andreas's *Energy Efficient Motors*.

Efficiency of 3 Phase AC Motors		
HP	NEMA* Eff.	Maximum Eff
2	84.0	86.5
3	86.5	89.5
5	87.5	90.2
50	93.0	95.0

Rotating Transformers

I included the 50 hp size to show how incredibly efficient these motors can be. In the electric industry, the most efficient device made is the transformer. It is used wherever wires are found: on poles in local streets as well as in the transmission of electricity at extremely high voltages. They are used to raise or reduce the AC voltage. Transformers attain efficiency levels of 99%. So, it has to be the ultimate compliment for 3 phase AC motors to be referred to as "rotating transformers."

Using 3 Phase AC Motors

Although the 3 phase AC motor has outstanding characteristics, there are a few problems to be resolved before this type of motor can be attached to batteries and linked to the propeller.

Standard Features

First, let us list the features which are standard and do not need to be modified:

The motors with a base are suitable for a pulley drive and can be mounted on any flat surface. This is the type used for an inboard drive. The "C" face end-mounted motors can be attached to an interface plate and the motor shaft connected to a coupling, which in turn can be connected to the shaft in the leg of an outboard motor.

The speed of the motor is controlled by the inverter/controller, which generates the 3 phase AC power and changes the frequency for speed control. As long as the speed is in the range of 1200 to 2000 rpm, the motor runs at its rated efficiency.

The shaft size and the motor size and weight are equal to or better than that of a DC motor.

These motors have excellent starting torque, more than enough to start the rotation of a propeller.

Three wires go to the motor, one for each phase; reversing the motor rotation is accomplished within the controller by interchanging two of the three phases.

Modifications Needed

Small 3 phase AC motors in the 2 to 5 hp range normally operate at 230/460 volts 60 cycles. Our motor would have to be rewound to operate at a battery voltage of 24 to 48 volts. (Only the "stator" requires rewinding; the rotor does not have to be modified in any way.)

An inverter/controller must be designed with the following functions and features:

It has to provide 3 phase AC power at a maximum of 150 amps for starting and 60 amps for continuous operation.

The frequency of the AC power has to be adjustable within a range of 40 to 70 cycles per second to control the speed of the motor.

Circuitry in the inverter/controller must be provided to turn the motor on and off and to make the motor operate in reverse.

3 Phase AC Motor Stator

The 3 phase AC induction motor has only two parts: a rotor and a stator. The only moving part is the rotor. The stator is shown in Photo 7.1.

Photo 7.1 3 Phase AC motor. Rewound Stator

To change the operating voltage of the motor, the stator must be rewound. No changes need to be made to the rotor. (Photo 9.3 compares an AC rotor with a DC armature).

Results of the DC Motor Survey

The DC motor survey was undertaken to find a better motor for the propulsion of boats. The desired improvements were: mostly greater efficiency and if possible, smaller size and lighter weight. The motors had to operate in the 24 to 48 volt battery voltage and generate 2 to 4 horsepower.

Nothing new or of great value was discovered. The "traction" motor, series wound golf cart motor, came out on top as the best value: an excellent GE 3 hp motor is available for about $400. Unfortunately, one has to live with an efficiency of less than 80% at full power and considerably less than that at a lower "cruising power."

At the time of the survey, the best motor for boating applications was the Lynch motor which uses a commutator and permanent magnets to obtain close to 90% efficiency at low battery voltage and low speed but at the much higher cost of over $1200.

Today, this same basic motor is built in China and is competitive in price with the golf cart motor. It is now found in many other applications such as outboard motors, robots and electric racing bicycles. It is an excellent choice for powering a boat in the 19 to 23 foot size.

My interest in finding an efficient, mass produced boat motor led me to the development of a 3 phase AC motor that ran on batteries. From the survey and my research, I knew that I would not find anything close to this motor "off the shelf". The two main problems being: the low battery voltage and the lack of an available three phase inverter/controller.

Test Equipment for Motor development Measuring the Output Power of a Motor

Before moving on to a description of the development and testing of the AC motor for boating applications in the next chapter, let's review the 2 basic pieces of test equipment needed to do this work.

The dynamometer is simply a device capable of measuring the output power of a motor. The old physics books generally described this type of device as a "Prony brake". It has a spring scale to measure the torque produced by the motor under test. What we're after is the torque in ft-lbs and the speed in revolutions per minute because we know that 1 hp is equal to 33,000 ft-lbs per minute.

The Prony brake works somewhat like the drum brake on a car. It consists of a large flat pulley with a leather belt around it. In theory, by adjusting the tension on the belt, the drag can be adjusted and measured on the spring scale. The sketch shown in the box below gives a general idea of the operation of this device.

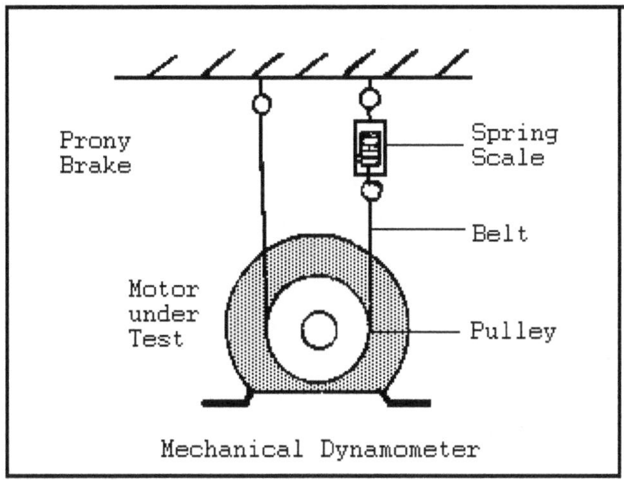

Mechanical Dynamometer

The horsepower of the device under test is determined in the following manner: if the pulley were 1 ft in diameter and the motor ran at 2000 rpm and produced 10 lbs of force on the spring scale, using the formula for hp, it would produce 1x3.14x2000x10 divided by 33,000 or 1.9 hp of output power.

I built such a device. However, there were two main problems. First, the pulley got very hot very fast. To be somewhat practical, the pulley would have to be water-cooled, a difficult feat to accomplish without splashing water all over the floor. The second problem was that the vibration created by the braking action made it very difficult to obtain a consistent reading on the spring scale. My advice is to forget all about it.

Using an Electric Brake

Instead of using a friction brake, attaching a generator to the shaft of the motor under test to perform the braking action worked much better. The field current of the generator can be controlled in order to increase or decrease the drag. In order to measure the torque, the generator was mounted on bearings, which allowed the generator to twist as the power was applied. A spring scale was then attached to an arm extending from the generator to measure the amount of twisting force in pounds.

Finding the necessary parts to build a dynamometer was not easy, but finding a dynamometer to buy was not easy either. Before building my own, I inquired at various rewinding shops for a supplier of these devices. I did find a used one at a good price, but it weighed 600 lbs.

While I was researching the market for dynamometers, it occurred to me that after World War II, all sorts of war surplus devices were converted to useful equipment. Back then, I had bought a B-29 aircraft generator to build an electric welder according to plans from *Popular Mechanics*. The welder never worked very well, but I had saved the generator. It had been in my basement for more than forty years but after cleaning it up, I found that it still worked. I still had the rheostat to control the field current, so all I needed was a resistive load. One of the golf cart speed control resistors turned out to be just the right size.

Photo 7.2 Dynamometer with 2 hp Motor under Test

Balancing the generator on its shaft was accomplished with a pillow block in front and a shaft extension in the rear. Photo 7.2 shows the converted aircraft generator connected to the 2 hp motor ready for testing.

Any generator can be turned into a dynamometer. The main requirement is that it can generate about 2000 watts at a speed of about 2000 rpm. An automobile alternator or generator would have to deliver about 180 amps at 12 volts to generate 2000 watts, which may be asking too much. A DC motor can also be made to operate as a generator but adjusting the field current is a problem in a series wound motor. Shunt wound DC motors in the 2 or 3 hp range would be a very good choice, but they are not easy to find.

The arm length from the center of the shaft to the spring scale connection shown in the picture was 8 inches. I reduced it from 12 inches to make it easier to read the spring scale. Under those conditions, the formula to determine the output power in watts is: 0.095 x rpm x lbs. To find the efficiency, the output power is divided by the input power. The input power in watts is the current multiplied by the voltage supplied to the motor. More details about the construction of a dynamometer are found in Part 3, Chapter 15.

The Oscilloscope

The only way to check out the operation of the electronics or to troubleshoot problems is with an oscilloscope. A "scope" is simply a device that shows the progress of an electric voltage over a period of time. If we were to scope the plus side of a 48 volt battery, we would see a straight line a certain distance above the 0 volt line in the plus direction. This indicates that this DC voltage does not change in value over time.

If we were to scope the output of a 110 volt AC outlet in the house, we would see a sine wave going above and below the 0 volt line. By adjusting the controls, we could determine that one full wave occurs every one sixtieth of a second. Many more functions like these are available on a basic scope.

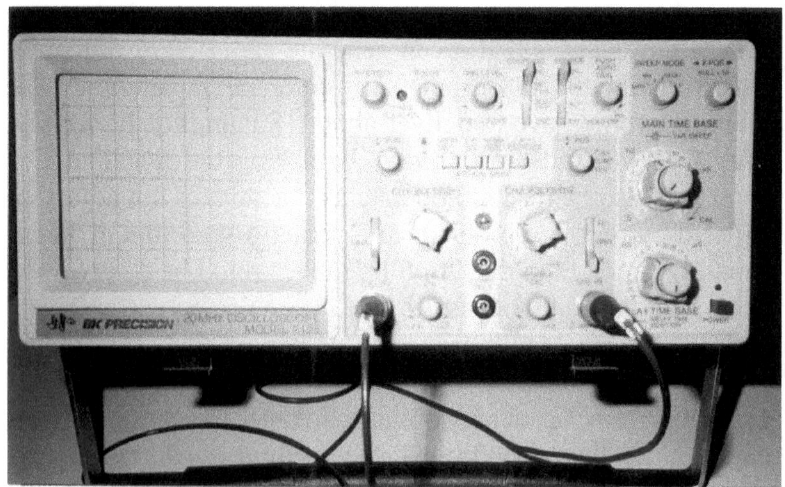

Photo 7.3 Dual Trace 20 Mhz Oscilloscope

The impressive array of switches and knobs that we see in photo 7.3 are used to control the amplitude and speed of the trace on the face of the scope. This scope has 2 traces which makes it somewhat more complex. It also has an extensive circuitry to "synch" (trigger, start) on various signals.

Let us consider one example. In the inverter/controller electronics (also known as the "logic"), you may want to trigger (start the trace going across the screen) on the signal that tells top switch "a" to close. Then with the second probe you would be able to check the timing of all the signals on the other phases to determine how they relate, time-wise, to the trigger signal.

Cost of the Oscilloscope

The cost of oscilloscopes goes up dramatically as the frequency bandwidth of the scope increases. For motor design applications, the minimum frequency available is more than adequate. Today, that would be a scope with a bandwidth of 20 Mhz. In such a scope, the fastest scale would be .05 microsecond. This means that a pulse one twentieth of a millionth of second long would be displayed on a centimeter division of the screen. That's very fast but compared to today's PC's which have a clock speed of more than 2 Ghz (the clock pulses occurring every 1/2 nanoseconds or 1/2 of a billionth of a second) it is barely idling!

New, a 20 Mhz dual trace scope costs about $600. Scopes are readily available on the used market where I found one at half price. The fellow who was selling it surprised me by telling me that he was a musician. He wanted to develop some sort of synthesized music and his girlfriend had bought him the scope for his birthday. The idea did not work, the girlfriend left him, and he needed money. I don't believe that he ever took the time to figure out how a scope really worked, but it was a good deal for me.

CHAPTER 8

Electric Motor Theory

Introduction

We have considered a few practical ideas to select an efficient boat hull and an efficient drive and propeller for an electric boat. In this chapter, we examine two types of electric motors, which are suited to power the boat.

The Thomas Register or its equivalent *ThomasNet* on line contains an incredible assortment of products and manufacturers. Under "electric motors" from "AC" to "waterproof," there are more than 200 pages with an average of fifty manufacturers and products per page. That's a total of 10,000 different motors, manufacturers and associated equipment.

You would think that in a universe that large there would be a good selection of efficient motors to power a boat. I selected twenty of the most promising candidates and wrote to the manufacturers using the set of criteria described at the beginning of Chapter 7. This exercise yielded a minimal amount of useful results. I found that motors are designed and built for specific applications and for the boating application, there is apparently nothing closer than the golf cart motor. Consequently, out of this very large assortment of motors, only two types will be reviewed: one includes the DC series motor and the Etek motor and the other includes the 3 phase AC induction motor.

Motor Basics

Motor rotation and torque are developed in a motor by the magnetic forces that come to bear on the rotating element of the motor--namely the armature in a DC motor and the rotor in an AC motor.

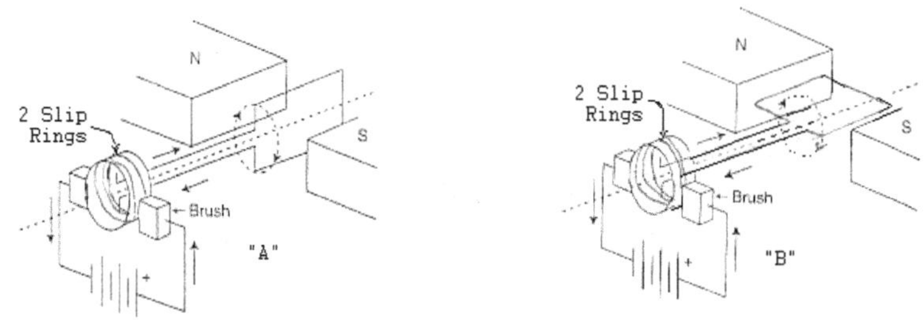

Simplified Armature in Positions "A" and "B"

The diagram above shows how these forces are developed. It also shows the need for a commutator to achieve continuous rotation. The "A" part of the diagram shows a simplified armature capable of rotating within a magnetic field produced by two magnets. Let's assume that the wire represents the winding of the armature. If it were in the vertical position when the circuit is turned on, it would turn to the horizontal position shown in "B" after the current starts flowing. The reason for this movement is that a magnetic field is generated around the wire due to the current flowing in it. Depending on the direction of the current flow, the wire will be attracted to the north or the south pole of the magnet.

There are two basic problems with this elementary device. First, it does not self-start from any position, and second it stops rotating as soon as the coil comes in close proximity to the magnet.

To make the motor start from whatever point it happened to stop is easy; several windings are wound on the armature so that one close to the magnet will cause the motor to start rotating.

To obtain continuous rotation requires the addition of the commutator. Its function is to reverse the flow of current (and therefore reverse the polarity of the magnetic field induced by the current in the wire) at the right time in order to be attracted to a magnet of the opposite polarity.

The diagram below shows that the slip rings were replaced by split rings that provide commutation by reversing the flow of current when the wire is in a vertical position. Photo 8.1 shows a DC armature with a 32 segment commutator.

The DC Motors

The type of DC motor that is best suited for use in electric boats is the series motor. It is available in the popular 2 to 4 hp size for applications such as golf carts sold by the hundreds of thousands every year. Other suitable DC motors are the shunt and the permanent magnet motor.

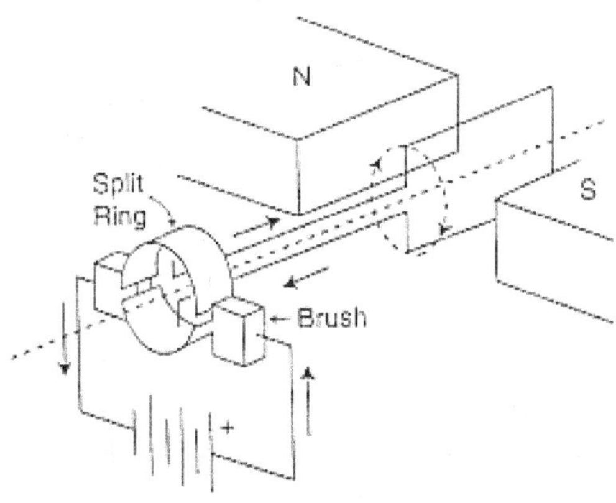

Split Ring Commutator

The DC Series Motor

The main characteristics of the DC series motor are excellent starting torque, good efficiency and good speed control. The series motor is also known as a traction motor due to its superior starting torque. The excellent starting torque feature is far less important in turning a propeller than in starting the motion of a golf cart since there is hardly any water resistance at very low propeller speeds. Reversing the direction of the motor is somewhat of a problem because either the armature current or the field current (but not both) must be reversed. Since all the current to the motor must be reversed, a heavy duty double pole, double throw relay is needed to accomplish this function.

The Shunt DC Motors

There are other DC motor configurations. One is the shunt motor where the field is connected to the battery in parallel with the armature instead of in series. Such motors exhibit less starting torque (which isn't really needed) and efficiencies that are equal to, or better than, the series motor. The shunt motor also has the advantage of providing speed control by adjusting the field current. Since the field current is far less than the armature current (unlike the series motor where they are equal), this motor requires lighter duty components. For the same reason, it is easier to reverse the direction of rotation in these motors. Unfortunately, because of low demand, these motors are not readily available.

The Permanent Magnet Motor

A third possibility is the permanent magnet (PM) motor. The motor field is replaced by permanent magnets to produce the required magnetic field. Because electric power is not needed to produce the magnetic field, the PM motor is by nature more efficient. There are some downsides to the use of permanent magnets. They are susceptible to demagnetization and to decreased magnetization as the temperature increases.

The Lynch Motor (Lynch Motors Co., London, England) is the perfect PM motor for boating applications. It has an outstanding efficiency close to 90%. In addition, a 3 hp motor weighs less than 30 lbs, and at 24 volts it operates at 1800 rpm. Operationally, the only negative is that the speed increases as the voltage increases. At 48 volts, for instance, the speed is 3600 rpm. A reduction gear would be necessary to operate the propeller at reasonable speed at this higher voltage. Another negative is the price of $1200.00, including shipping but without speed control. If price is not important, the Lynch Motor is a very good candidate. Interestingly, this motor is designed specifically for a boating application. To my knowledge, it is the only one that is.

The Rhodes 19 which was converted into an electric boat in Chapter 6 using the Etek motor (a direct descendent of the Lynch motor) gave excellent results with a direct drive and a PWM (Pulse Width Modulation) Curtis controller with 36 volt batteries.

The Commutator

A significant negative feature of all DC motors is the need for a commutator . The commutator is expensive to build, and the brushes require maintenance. The sparking can also be a problem in explosive environments and it can interfere with the operation of electronic equipment. The power required to overcome the friction of the brushes reduces the efficiency as we saw in the no-load tests that were performed on several DC and AC motors. Over the years these problems have been minimized but they are still troublesome.

Armature and Commutator of DC Motor
Photo 8.1

The DC Series Motor's Characteristics

We will look at the important characteristics of the DC series motor by examining performance curves. We will also discuss the auxiliary equipment needed for speed control to start, stop and reverse the direction of the motor.

The DC series motor is an average performer in terms of efficiency, but availability and reasonable cost (about $500.00) makes it a good candidate to power electric boats.

The curves shown in Figure 12.1 indicate the horsepower and the efficiency of a typical DC series motor. These were provided by the manufacturer for a GE 2 hp "JB" series motor running at 36 volts. (My own efficiency curves of a similar GE motor top out at a maximum of 74% rather than the 79% shown here.)

What these Curves Tell Us

The curves of the GE JB series motor shown in Figure 8.1. were provided by GE. They show the relationship between the current, the efficiency and the speed as a function of the torque (in pound-feet) produced by the motor. Since the torque is closely related to the hp, we can also visualize what happens to these three motor characteristics as a function of hp.

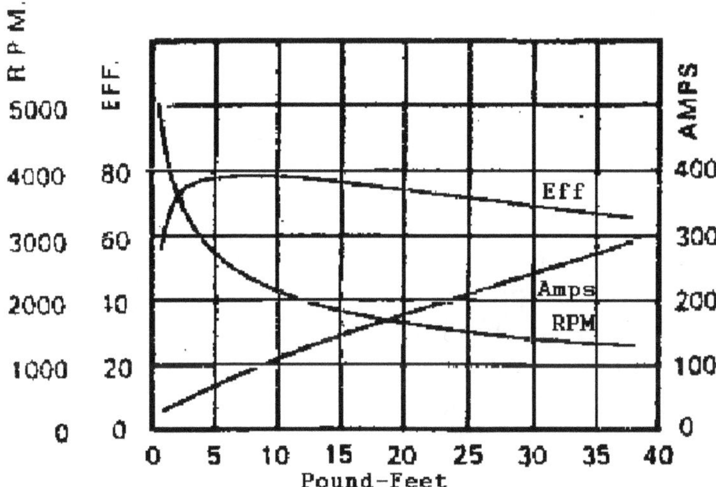

Figure 8.1 GE 2 hp "JB" Series DC 36 volt Motor

The most obvious observation to be derived from these curves is that the motor is far more powerful than is implied by its rating. For example, at maximum efficiency, the motor produces 10 ft-lbs of torque. At 2100 rpm, using the hp formula below, that figures out to be 4 hp, which is twice the rating of the motor:

$$hp = \frac{\text{Torque x 6.28 x RPM}}{33{,}000}$$

The curves also show that the motor is actually capable of producing 35 ft-lbs of torque, which is more than 8 hp or four times the motor's rating. The reason we can't use all this power is that the motor is not rated to run **continuously** at this level of output. Also, note that to generate this amount of power would require a current drain of 270 amps from a 36 volt battery pack.

Another observation that can be made from the curves is that the motor speed varies greatly as the power is increased. At 2 hp, the rated speed is 3300 rpm whereas at maximum torque of 35 ft lbs, the speed is 1300 rpm. This speed variation makes it difficult to select a propeller that provides the best combination of output power, speed and efficiency.

Accessories for the Series Motor Speed Control

The most important additional piece of equipment required to run the motor in a boat is the speed controller. Assuming that the propeller is selected to produce hull speed at maximum motor efficiency, it is only necessary to reduce the speed of the motor. That can only be done by reducing the battery voltage at the motor.

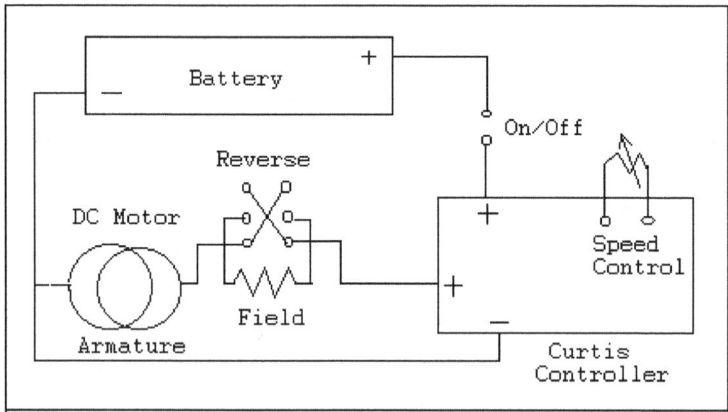

Block Diagram: DC Motor Control

There are many ways to reduce the battery voltage: a series resistance can be added to the motor circuit, the battery pack can be tapped at a lower voltage, but the most practical (and also the most expensive) is to use an electronic controller such as the Curtis Controller. A block diagram of the Curtis Controller is shown above. A wiring diagram of the controller with the on/off and reverse switches is shown in Part 3, Chapter 13.

This is a pulse width modulation (PWM) device that effectively reduces the battery voltage by chopping the output current into pulses of variable length (much more about PWM in Chapter 9)

On/Off and Reverse

A solenoid similar to the relay that turns on a car starter motor is required to start and stop the DC motor. It should be capable of handling 100 amps of current.

A double pole, double throw relay is needed to reverse the direction of the motor. It should also be capable of interrupting 100 amps. These devices are also shown in the block diagram and discussed in "Build it yourself" Chapter 13.

The 3 Phase AC Motor

Before reviewing the description and the operation of the 3 phase AC motor, a comparison between the two types of motor is shown in the chart on the next page. Only the multi-phase AC machines are considered. Single phase motors are easily available and are quite inexpensive. But single phase motors do not compare favorably with the 3 phase motors in terms of weight, reliability and efficiency.

The chart also lists the basic components of the DC motor system shown on the block diagram. An estimate of the cost is included. It is compared with the estimated cost of an equivalent 3 phase AC system.

The conclusion is that the 3 phase AC motor compares very favorably with the well established DC series motor. In fact, it is superior in every way except starting torque, which is not an issue in boating applications.

DC Series Motor vs. 3 Phase AC Motor

Characteristics	DC	3Phase AC
Weight	Average	Average
Size	Average	Average
Noise Level	Above Average	Less than Ave.
Starting Torque	Above Average	Average
Reliability	Average	Above Average
Cost of the Motor	$500	$250
Cost of the Controller	$300	$400
Cost of the Accessories (Start/Stop, Reverse)	$100	$0(Controller)

Operation of the 3 Phase AC Motor

As we have mentioned, the operation of the two types of motors is quite different. The DC motor generates its rotational torque by energizing a magnetic field in the armature next to the appropriate magnetic field in the stator. This selection process is performed by the commutator.

The AC induction motor on the other hand, uses the alternating feature of the AC power to produce a rotating magnetic field in the stator. The rotating field cuts across the bus bar imbedded in the rotor, thereby inducing a heavy current in the rotor. The heavy current, in turn, generates a magnetic field that attempts to catch up to the rotating magnetic field in the stator. It never quite makes it. If the speed of the rotor were to come close to that of the stator's rotating field, the induced current in the rotor would diminish and this would reduce the strength of the magnetic field in the rotor, causing it to slow down.

The right amount of slip between the rotor and the rotating magnetic field results in a state of equilibrium, which varies slightly depending on the load but is generally about 50 rpm: full speed is about 1750 rpm in a 4 pole motor.

The basic speed of a 2 pole, 3 phase AC motor is 3600

rpm minus a slip of about 100 rpm.

No Brushes Needed

The 3 phase AC motor's ability to operate without the need of a commutator and the attendant brushes is a major advantage. As we will see in Photo 9.3, the rotor of the AC motor is far simpler and less expensive to manufacture because it has neither brushes nor a commutator with copper windings connected to it.

The brushes required by the DC motor have always been a maintenance problem. Not only do they wear and cause the commutator to wear, but they create arcing that causes interference in electronic gear and can be a hazard in an explosive environment. The drag produced by the brushes is a significant deterrent to high efficiency.

Over the years, a great deal of effort has been expended to improve the commutation process. The carbon brushes themselves have been greatly improved to increase the wearing quality and decrease the arcing. Some brushes are now built so that the resistance of the carbon in the direction of the commutator segments is high whereas the resistance in the direction of the current is low.

The AC motor, on the other hand, with its single moving part on two ball bearings is the epitome of simplicity, reliability and efficiency.

Why Aren't the AC Motors Available?

So, if the AC motors are so great, why aren't they readily available for battery operated applications? The DC motor is still the product of choice and, to my knowledge, an equivalent AC motor with an inverter/controller is not available. I believe that the reason is a combination of the following:

Greater efficiency is not readily observed or

appreciated. In a golf cart application, for instance, better efficiency would mean that the cart would go farther between recharges. But if the batteries don't generally run down during the day, and they get recharged every night anyway, this advantage is of marginal value.

The lower cost of the AC motor in combination with its better efficiency and greater reliability should be a significant advantage. But it will require a considerable effort and expenditure to develop a low voltage inverter/controller and turn it into a dependable commercial product.

There is no doubt that the existing 3 phase motor design can easily be adapted to battery operation (basically, just a lower voltage winding in the stator is needed), but the inverter/controller would be a brand new device to be developed and thoroughly tested.

Existing 3 phase motors with inverter/controllers are designed for 230/460 volt operation. The transistor switching circuits used in these devices reduce the efficiency of the motor by less than 1% at 460 volts. Using these same transistor switching devices at 48 volts would reduce the efficiency of the motor by close to 8%. Since this is not acceptable, a new switching device would have to be developed. From the results that I have obtained, the Mosfet devices can do the switching easily and efficiently. However, the circuitry that I developed is in the "laboratory curiosity" stage of development. Much more testing is needed.

As long as the manufacturers supplying DC motors are not pressed to build a better product, why should they spend the time and money to develop something so radically different? Not being in the electronics design business, they probably lack the competence to design such a product even though it is closely allied with the operation of their motors. Notice, for instance, how the market is fragmented: motor control devices are not built by motor manufacturers but by a totally different group of electronics manufacturers.

Conclusions

1. A properly designed 3 phase AC motor has many advantages over the traditional DC series motor in marine propulsion applications.

2. There is little incentive for the present manufacturers to produce an AC counterpart to the DC motor because it would require a development effort in electronics where they are not skilled.

3. In due time, the continued decrease in the price of the electronics and the continued increase in the price of copper and of the complex machining needed to build the commutator will lead someone to bite the bullet and build a better motor.

Since the speed control is practically free when a 3 phase inverter/controller is built, I picture the controller being built into the motor (as it is in hand tools). The Mosfet switches could be built into the frame of the motor as the diodes of a car alternator are built in their frame. Such a motor would not require any external components for the generation of the 3 phase AC and would have a built-in speed controller.

Summary of the Contents Of the Next Chapter

Over the next couple of years, I would rewind three motors, a one, a three and then a two hp motor in order to run them on battery power. Some of these motors were rewound more than once. To generate the three phase AC power, I designed and built ten different 3 phase AC inverter/controllers before getting it right.

In the first edition of this book, this very tedious work is described in five chapters. In this edition, I have condensed the relevant information in the next very long chapter by using the three hp AC motor as an example to explain how an AC motor can be run on batteries. This chapter explores the following elements of the AC motor and its controller:

The basics of generating square waves from DC as opposed to AC sine waves are explained.

The 3 sections which make up the inverter/controller are explained using simple block diagrams.

The need to rewind the motor to operate on battery voltage is explained and a simple formula to determine the number of turns and the size of the wire is presented.

The many iterations needed to obtain the final version of an operational inverter/ controller are described.

Finally, a big test at Mort Ray's shop comparing the 3 phase AC motor with his production DC motor is described and the results obtained are discussed.

After the completion of the big test, further efficiency improvements were contemplated using a 2 hp AC motor. The motor was rewound twice and was connected to a computer controlled inverter/controller to smooth out the square wave along with other tests.

I hope that the technically minded readers will enjoy my successes and tribulations as much as I did.

CHAPTER 9

The 3 Phase AC Motor

Running an AC Motor on Batteries

My first attempt at building an inverter/controller to run an AC motor from batteries was most deliberate. I did not know whether the idea had any merit and I did not plan to bet the farm on it.

First, I had to get a motor. I visited the local motor rewinding shop and came away with a burnt-out 1 hp Lincoln 230/460 volt, 3 phase, 60 cycle motor. I think the owner gave it to me so I'd go away and not ask any more questions.

When I took the motor apart, I found that the rear bearing had seized and had rotated in its enclosure to the point where it enlarged the socket sufficiently to let the rotor rub against the stator. At some point the rotor must have locked up and burned out the windings. I found a replacement bearing and after wrapping it with a thin shim, I pressed it solidly back into place. The rotor turned freely and, although this wasn't a permanent repair, I hoped it would work well enough to test out the idea. The burned-out windings did not matter since the motor would be rewound for the lower battery voltage.

Building an Inverter/Controller

The next step was to build a basic inverter/controller. All I wanted at this point was to generate the 3 phase AC. I wanted to transform the DC from the battery into AC, and I wanted to be able to control the frequency of the AC in order to control the speed of the motor.

An inverter/controller is built in three sections. In order

to limit the interference created by the switching section, it is built on three separate circuit boards as described below:

1. The timing section generates the 60 cycle AC and controls the frequency (which, in turn, controls the speed of the motor).
2. The control section generates the 3 phase square waves and controls the operation of the motor (start/stop, reverse, safety circuits).
3. The switching section provides the power to run the motor.

The description below, call it "Inverters 101," touches on the high points of the theory of AC inverters. At this point, the description does become a bit more technical and may require a couple of rereads. There are few other concepts in this book that are difficult to grasp. A basic understanding of electricity will help understand this section. An excellent book on the basics of electricity is Miner Brotherton's *"The 12 volt Bible for Boats"*

Basics of AC Square Waves The H Switch

A good way to explain how DC is transformed (inverted) into AC is to consider the operation of an H switch (see box below). As the diagram shows, there are four switches: two of them are connected to the plus (+) side of the battery and two of them are connected to the minus (--) side of the battery. (There is a convention of sorts that uses the subscript "t" [for "top"] for the switches connected to the plus side of the battery and the subscript of "b" [for "bottom"] for the switches connected to the minus side of the battery. We will use that convention). Where the bar across the H would normally be is where the load is connected. The two circles represent a motor.

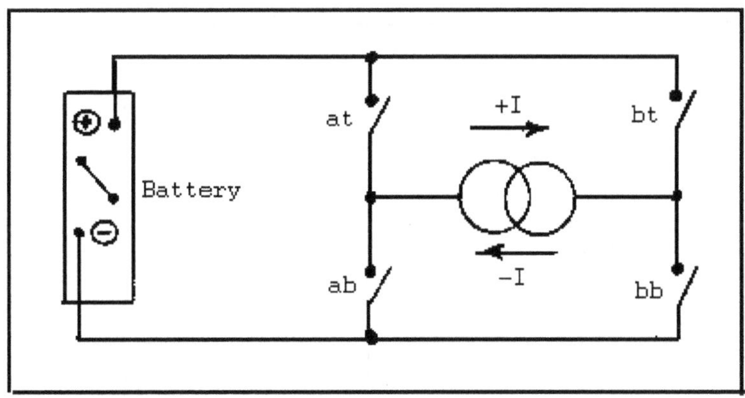

H Switch Diagram

The operation of the H switch is as follows: when switches at and bb are closed, positive current (I+) flows through the motor. On the other hand, when switches ab and bt are closed, negative current (I--) flows through the motor. So, if we were to plot this sequence of events (the current over a certain time period), it would look like the square-wave in the box below (shown as a solid line).

The plot shows "current" on the vertical axis and "time" on the horizontal axis. At point A, the first two switches close, at point B the first two switches open and the next two switches close and at point C the last two switches reopen.

Assuming that the switches shown in the diagram were controlled electronically, they would operate very fast. The whole sequence of events would take place in 1/60 of a second. The dotted line in the shape of a sine wave represents one cycle of 60 cycle AC power from the power company. As we can see, there is a resemblance between the square wave generated by the inverter switches and the sine wave generated by the power company. A single phase AC inverter works in this manner.

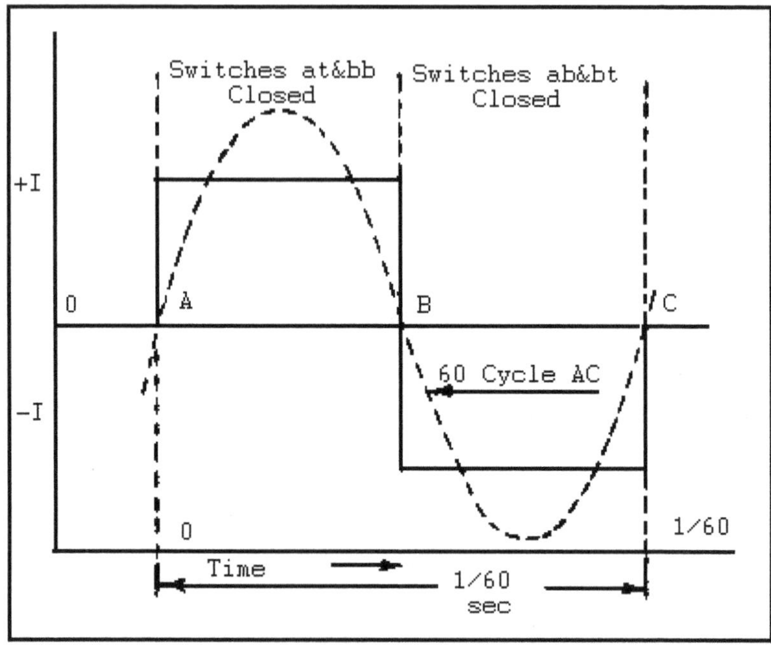

Square Wave (Current vs Time)

3 Phase Switching

At this point, it isn't hard to guess that by adding more switches, we should be able to simulate a 3 phase power source. A 3 phase switching diagram, using six switches instead of four, is shown in the box below.

Here, we have the battery connected to three pairs of switches (just one more pair than single phase AC). The additional switches are ct and cb. The common connection between each pair of switches is wired to one phase of the 3 phase motor. 3 phase AC devices can be connected in one of two ways: either in "delta" or in "wye." For now, we will observe that the motor is connected in delta.

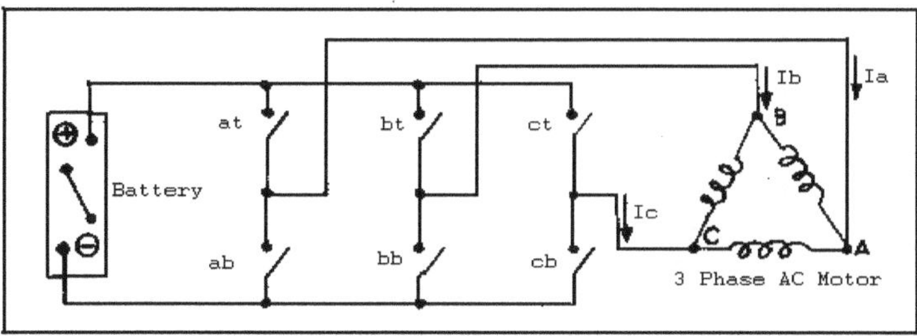

3 Phase Switching Diagram

A Note of Caution

This is a good time to make an important observation. **Of all the different combinations of pairs of switches which close simultaneously in both the simple H switch and the 3 phase switch configuration, top and bottom switches of the same phase, such as at and ab, must never close at the same time.** Looking at the switching diagram, we can see that such an action would put a direct short across the battery resulting in the catastrophic destruction of the switches. (I have hundreds of blown out electronic circuits to prove this point.) Some of this destruction was due to my own stupidity, but in most cases it was due to "glitches" in the electronics. Most of the time, the cause was an electrical noise which was generated when the high currents were switched on and off.

So called "anti-ambiguity" circuits , which prevent two switches of the same phase from closing at the same time should be included in this type of circuitry. I found out the hard way that this precaution is essential.

The Current within the Motor Windings

The simplified switching diagram in the middle of the drawing below shows the same six power switches and the common connection of each pair of switches to the input of the motor at points A, B and C discussed above.

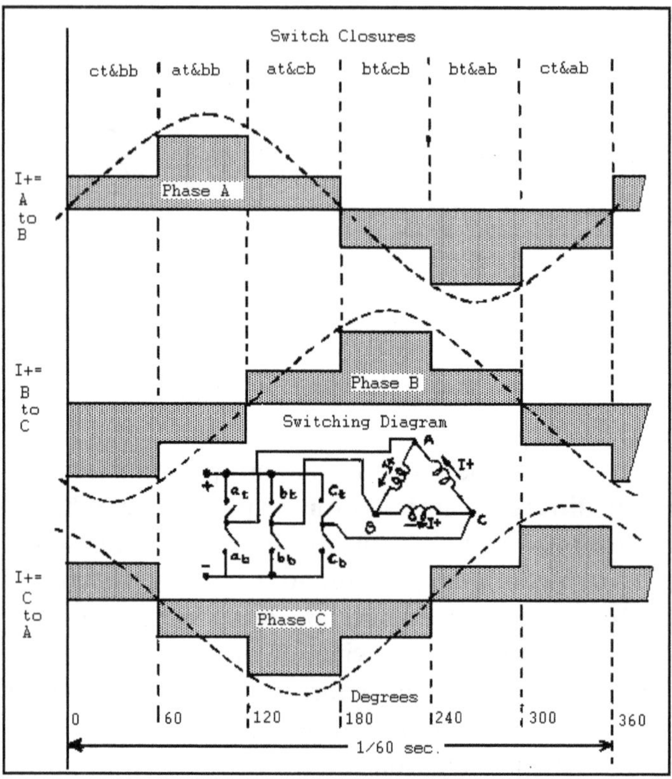

Current through the Motor Windings

We won't go through the tedious exercise of following the flow of current to the motor windings during the closure of each pair of switches (as I did in the first edition of this book). It should be evident that three square waves can be generated by dividing a 1/60 of a second into six more 30 degree subdivisions.

The remarkable similarity between the square wave pattern shown here and the 3 phase sine wave pattern from the power company is the reason why the 3 phase inverters work so well.

Amazing Speed of the Electronics

When one considers that in a four pole, 3 phase AC motor spinning at 1800 rpm, all these switches closing and opening and all these currents increasing and decreasing happen during 1/2 of one revolution, it is mind boggling. On the other hand, compared to the speed of today's slowest personal computer, this is the equivalent of a trip on the proverbial slow boat to China as opposed to going by jet.

We should also remember that the current flowing through each turn of each winding must have the proper additive effect. Each coil shown in the simplified diagram is, in reality, six windings. When the motor is wound, the correct number of turns must be placed in each of the 36 slots and the current must enter and exit each winding in the correct clockwise or counterclockwise direction. Fortunately, the very clever motor engineers solved this problem for us long ago.

The Operation of the Inverter/Controller

To activate the six switches that generate the 3 phase square waves, which, in turn, simulate the 3 phase power from the electric company, three functions must be implemented by the inverter/controller:

1. A timing section must generate six signals every cycle at frequencies adjustable from 40 to 72 cycles per second. These frequencies produce motor speeds of 1200 to 2200 rpm.

2. A control section must generate three sets of square waves 120 degrees apart. The control section must also start and stop the motor and cause it to operate in forward or reverse. Several safety features must also be implemented in this section, such as under-voltage protection, over-current protection and the previously mentioned anti-ambiguity circuits.

3. A switching section, which will accept the signals from the control section and activate the switch drivers that control the high power Mosfet switches.

My latest implementation of each of these functions is explained below.

The First of Many Inverter/Controllers

The first inverter/controller that I built for the 1 hp motor required 15 TTL ICs (Integrated Circuits) without the implementation of any protective circuits. It was unduly complex because I was unaware of the six step sequence of switch closures that simulate the 3 phase AC waveform at that time. Instead, I divided each $1/60^{th}$ second cycle into 100 parts and turned the six switches on and off with a minimum leeway of one hundredth of a cycle. Decoding each of these twelve operations was a tedious task and the close switching tolerances were not conducive to a long and healthy life for the electronic power switches.

It did work as planned. I still turn the electronics on occasionally because it has a neat feature. I added an LED (light emitting diode) to each of the six switches and arranged them in a circle. By slowing the timing unit way down, each light comes on one after the other as they go around in a circle.

These blinking lights going around and around are significant because this is exactly how a 3 phase AC induction motor works: the magnetic field goes around and around the stator, inducing a magnetic field in the rotor which effectively drags the rotor around on its shaft. In the DC motor, on the other hand, the correct motor winding is selected by the cummutator to attract a winding (or a magnet) of the correct polarity.

Rewinding the 1 hp Motor
Basic Characteristics of Small AC Motors

Most small 3 phase AC motors (less than 5 hp) are wired for 230/460 volts AC. Each phase has two sets of 6 windings. For 230 volt operation, the windings are connected in parallel. For 460 volt operation, the windings are connected in series.

These motors are available in two basic speeds: a nominal 1800 rpm for a four pole motor and a nominal 3600 rpm for a two pole motor. We need the 1800 rpm version because we want the propeller speed to be as slow as possible with as little gear reduction as possible. I planned to rewind the motor exactly the same way as it was wired for 230 volt operation.

The Lincoln 1 hp motor had 68 turns of number 24 wire in each slot. All told there are 36 slots to be divided among the 3 phases. The windings were carefully removed and the location of each winding was carefully documented.

Calculating the Number of Turns Per Slot

There is a lot more to the calculation of the number of turns needed for a lower voltage application than what I did for this motor. Here, I divided the rated voltage of 230 volts by the 30 volt battery voltage that I wanted to use, obtaining a ratio of 8 to 1. Then by dividing the number of turns (68) by this ratio, I obtained 8.5. This was the number of turns needed to run the motor at 30 volts. I rounded this number out to 8 turns per slot.

Calculating the Wire Size

The same ratio of 8 to 1 was used to determine the size of the wire. The new winding would carry eight times as much current as the original (thereby keeping the ampere-turns the same), so a much heavier wire than the original number 24 wire was needed.

As the number associated with wire size gets smaller, the wire gets heavier. A wire three sizes smaller than 24, namely number 21, has exactly twice the area and therefore can carry twice as much current as the number 24 wire. To carry eight times the current, we needed a wire nine sizes smaller than 24, namely number 15 wire. Odd numbered sized wire is not as readily available as the even sized wire. Moreover, the more copper that is used, the less the heat loss and the more efficient the motor. After making sure that it would fit in the slot, I decided to use 8 turns of the heavier number 14 wire. From all the rounding and estimating that I did, it can be concluded that this is not an exact science.

This first rewinding job was agonizingly slow but it came out very well. The rotor turned freely and there were no short circuits that I could detect. Coupled with Proto 1, my first inverter/controller, I was at last ready to test the concept of a 3 phase AC motor running on battery power.

Performance Results of the 1 hp Motor

The rewound 1 hp motor was connected to Proto #1's power switches. Starting at a very low voltage of 6 volts, the power was turned on and the motor ran. I soon found out that 24 volts was the highest voltage that the switches could withstand; consequently, the motor did not attain its full power rating.

Performance of the Rewound 1 HP AC Motor			
Speed	Current at 24 volts	HP Output	Efficiency
1300RPM	22.0 Amps	.46 HP	67%
1400RPM	22.5 Amps	.50 HP	72%
1650RPM	30.0 Amps	.59 HP	64%

Although this first inverter/controller was far from a refined product, it did power the 1 hp motor to approximately 1/2 of its rated output at speeds from 1300 to 1650 rpm. The average efficiency was approximately 68%. The results shown in the box above were very encouraging.

There was no question that the inverter/controller worked. The real question was, could it outperform the efficiency of a DC motor of the same power which had been undergoing refining for the last 100 years?

The Second Prototype

At this point, I had discovered the advantages of a 6 count counter for the clock. I built a second inverter/controller using the integrated circuit (IC) MC33033. This change alone reduced the IC count from 15 to 10 and reduced the rat's nest of interconnecting wires to a more acceptable number.

The results of using Proto 2 to run the 1 hp motor were very similar to the results obtained in the previous experiment. When I tried to raise the voltage above 24 volts, I succeeded only in blowing another handful of Mosfet switching devices. I was making progress, but I wanted to turn the baby steps into giant strides. Little did I know that it would take the better part of two summers before I would have an inverter/controller that could switch the hoped for 150 amps at 48 volts (10 hp) without difficulty.

A New Start

I decided that all parts of the AC motor project needed improvement: the motor, the logic and the switching circuits.

The Lincoln 1 hp motor that I used did not have an efficiency rating on the nameplate but by researching some catalogs, I estimated that it was probably 75%. I reasoned that I could make a 15% improvement in the efficiency by starting with a premium 3 hp motor with an efficiency factor in the 90% range.

The logic of the inverter/controller needed to be simplified and enhanced with control and safety features. The switching circuits needed the most work. By failing at voltages higher than 24 volts, the motor could not operate at its rated power level. I decided to start over with a new motor and newly designed electronics.

I bought the new AC motor, a 3 hp Dayton "wattrimer" from W.W. Grainger for less than $200.00. At 56 lbs the motor weighed a little more than I had expected, but since I planned to use it in the inboard configuration of *Sunny*, it did not matter. The most attractive features were the high efficiency (90.2%) and the low price. To obtain this high efficiency, I also needed a new inverter/controller and a better switching section. I also needed to rewind the motor for 48 volt battery operation. We consider each of these requirements later in this chapter.

The operation of the logic is explained in general terms with the use of block diagrams. The chapters with the actual logic diagrams and wiring schedules shown in the first edition of the book are deleted in this edition.

Developing a New Inverter/Controller Desirable Features

Proto 3 incorporated the lessons learned with prototypes 1 and 2 and included features that were needed but not yet designed. An important step was to incorporate the Motorola MC33033 chip in the design. The MC33035 is used in later prototypes but its specifications are too close to the MC33033's to differentiate between the two. A list of useful features described in the specifications include:

Under-voltage protection
Over-current protection
Forward/Reverse
Coasting (to turn the motor on and off)
Pulse Width Modulation (PPM for added speed control)

It turned out that these features were not easy to implement. My biggest disappointment was the inability to use the forward/reverse feature of the chip. Because the 33033 is designed for the control of brushless DC motors, the reversal of 2 of the 3 phases, which is needed to put a 3 phase AC motor in reverse, is not implemented. Reverse had to be implemented with additional IC's instead of using the 33033.

The over-current and PWM (pulse width modulation) features worked marginally well. They were both very susceptible to electrical noise and gave me mixed results depending on the proximity of the high current wiring. Nevertheless, I implemented the new inverter/controller with the 33033 chip hoping to overcome these deficiencies at a later time.

Cross Talk

Up to this point, I had used point to point wiring of the circuit board seeing that the circuits were prototypes which required changes and upgrades as I went along with the design. But I had seen many warnings about possible cross talk between wires that could cause jittery operation or, at worst, unintended switching actions which could destroy the power switches.

Cross talk is an induced signal in adjacent wires due to their proximity to one another. They affect the circuit's operation in the same manner as electrical noise. Proto 4 had the same design as Proto 3 except that I built it on a two-sided printed circuit board to avoid the cross talk. I can't say that I saw any noticeable improvement. The major problem of not being able to operate reliably at a voltage higher than 24 volts was still torturing me.

The next three sections briefly describe the circuits needed to generate 3 phase AC power by using a block diagram for each section, they are the timing, the control and the switching sections.

The Timing Section

The timing circuit is where the pulses, which control the entire operation, are created. It is the easiest to understand, making it a good place to start. The timing circuits did not change materially over the course of the design of the ten prototypes so I'll describe the final version used in Proto 10.

The timing section has three parts: the clock, the decoder and the isolators.

The clock is an all purpose chip available at Radio Shack capable of generating pulses at various frequencies. All that is needed is a 9 volt battery, a capacitor and a potentiometer of the appropriate size. By generating pulses at frequencies varying from 72,000 to 132,000 Hz (hertz or cycles per second), the resulting square waves cause a 3 phase AC, 1750 rpm motor to run at speeds ranging from 1200 to 2200 rpm. The potentiometer (just like the volume control of a stereo) would therefore, control the speed of the boat.

It may not seem that this limited rpm range is sufficient to control the speed of the boat but remember that the power output of the prop is a cube function: doubling the speed increases the output power by a factor of eight.

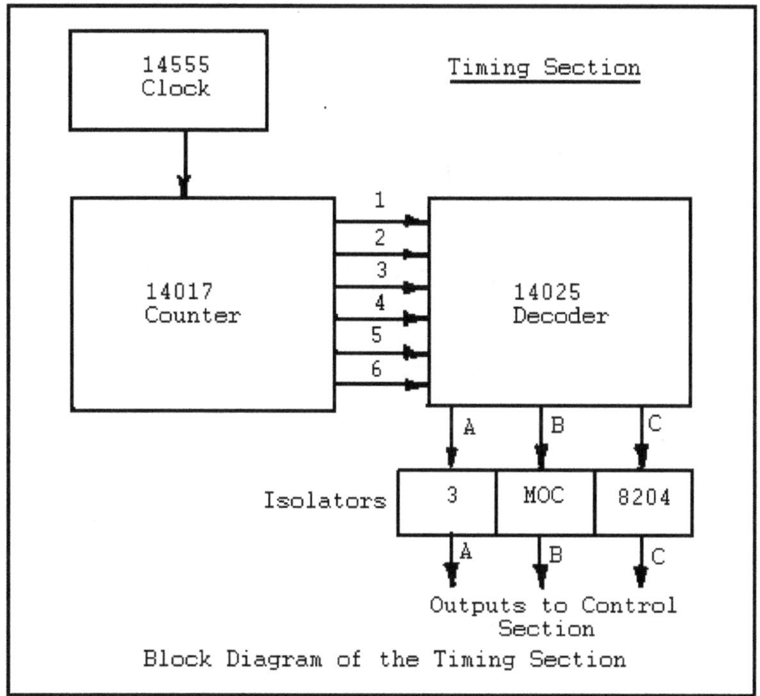

Block Diagram of the Timing Section

Two ICs were used to count up to six and to decode the square waves. These square waves met the input requirements of the MC33033 motor control IC.

The isolators were added to the circuit when the timing board was separated from the rest of the logic for packaging convenience. It also insured that the electrical noise generated by the switching section did not affect the operation of the timing circuits.

The Control Section

The control section circuits are shown in the block diagram below. The diagram shows that the pulses from the timing logic go to the 33033 motor control IC. The output of the 33033 chip goes to the level inverter, the forward/ reverse circuitry, the anti-ambiguity block and finally to the switch drivers.

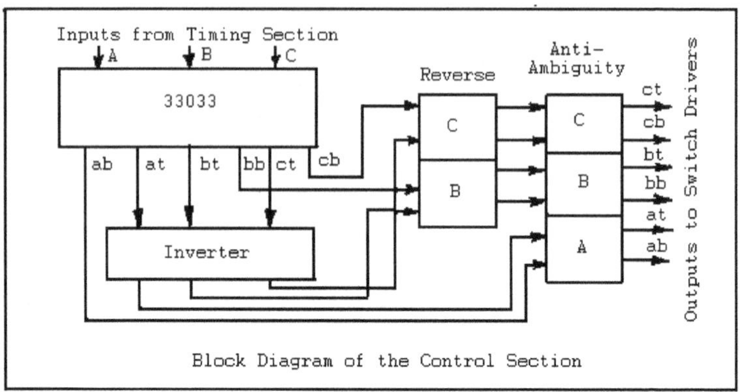

Block Diagram of the Control Section

The 33033 chip is capable of generating the correct pulses to drive a small 3 phase AC motor. For a 3 hp motor, where the switching currents will be in the order of 150 amps to start the motor, heavy duty switch drivers are needed. Between the 33033 and the switch drivers are three other boxes described below.

The level inverter is simply an inverter IC connected to the output of the 33033. An inverter is used to reverse the polarity of a level. For example, if a level goes from +12 volts to ground (as it does in this case), the level will go from ground (0 volts) to +12 volts after going through the inverter. It is required here because the output levels of the three top switches are opposite in polarity from the three bottom switches.

We've mentioned before that the forward/reverse feature of the 33033 does not work on 3 phase AC motors. The circuit shown here performs that function.

The circuits shown in the anti-ambiguity block implement a safety feature mentioned before: they prevent the unintentional operation of the circuit should two switches of the same phase close at the same time.

The Switching Section

As seen in the block diagram below, there are 3 switch drivers modules and 48 IRF540 Mosfets in the switching sections. The design of the switching circuits can get pretty technical and I did try a lot of different combinations of devices. Suffices to say that after much experimenting, I used the IR 2112 chip with its shut down feature in the final version of the inverter/controller. The IR 2112 is designed specifically to drive the N channel power Mosfet.

"Off-the-Shelf" Controllers

When I started experimenting with devices for high speed, high current electronic switching, I looked into the possibility of adapting existing off-the-shelf devices designed for this job. I found two: one was a 3 phase AC motor controller costing about $700.00 at W.W. Grainger and the other was a product called POW/RTRAIN made by International Rectifier (IR) at a cost of about $300.00. Both of these inverter/controllers were powered by a 230/460 volt 3 phase AC source. The AC was converted to DC, then the DC was inverted back to AC at a variable frequency to control the speed of the motor.

I didn't buy either of them because these devices operated at a much higher voltage than the battery voltage that I would be using. Consequently, the switches used in these devices are transistors, which have a 2 volt voltage drop when they are turned on. Since there were two switches for each phase, the total voltage loss was 4 volts. 4 volts out of 460 is less than a 1% loss, but 4 volts out of a battery voltage of 48 volts is more than an 8% loss, which was not acceptable.

It was reassuring to know that 3 phase AC inverters were used commercially to control the speed of large 3 phase AC motors (50 hp and over). One such application was the control of irrigation pumps for golf courses (pumps and propellers have very similar characteristics). I decided to look elsewhere for a more efficient electronic switch considering the importance that I was placing on very high overall efficiency.

Enter the Power Mosfet

The answer turned out to be a power Mosfet switching device that could replace the bipolar transistors mentioned above. The Mosfet is relatively new compared to the power transistor. Its main advantage in this application is that the voltage drop across the switch is far less than that of a transistor, thereby reducing the losses and greatly improving the efficiency. Its main disadvantage is that its rated operating voltage is far less than the transistor's. In this application, due to the low battery voltage, that is not a problem.

Mosfet switches come in many different types, characteristics, and packages. The two main suppliers are IR and Motorola. After much experimentation with N channel and P channel devices as well as the switch drivers needed to activate them, I settled on the IRF540N. It is rated at 100 volts, which provides a good deal of safety ("headroom" as it is sometimes called) when using a 48 volt battery. The current rating is 29 amps (232 amps with 8 in parallel). In the key efficiency department, the "on" resistance, as it is known, is 0.052 ohms. (It determines the voltage loss when the switch is turned on.) The last time I bought them, these Mosfets cost $1.12 each. They are among the least expensive Mosfets available. Today, the newer designs would cost more but with their higher rating, only 2 would be needed in parallel

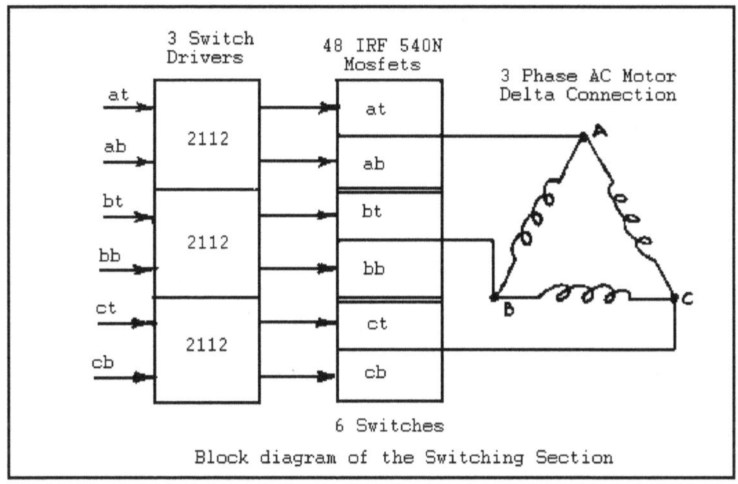

Block diagram of the Switching Section

The block diagram in the box above shows the final design of Proto 10. The six sets of switches (each one consists of eight Mosfets in parallel) were activated by the three switch drivers. The six switches were connected to the 3 phase AC motor, which is shown connected in delta.

With the electronics under control, the only thing left to do was rewind the motor.

Rewinding the 3 hp Motor

The Dayton 3 hp motor is a stock 3 phase AC high efficiency motor (the only kind being manufactured since October 1997). It is rated at 90.2% efficiency according to the nameplate. Like all 3 phase AC motors, it has a service factor of 115%, which means that it can be operated at 15% overload continuously. This makes it equivalent to a DC motor rated at 3.5 hp.

The 230/460 volt windings were carefully removed while recording the location and the direction (clockwise or counterclockwise) of each of the six coils of wire weaved in the 36 slots. There were 50 turns of double number 20 wire in each coil in the 230 volt configuration.

Since the plan was to operate the motor at 48 volts a ratio of 5 to 1 was used. The number of turns per slot was reduced from 50 to 10 and the size of the wire was increased from double #20 to double #14.

Preliminary Tests of the 3 hp Motor

Motor rewinding shops have an elaborate electronic device to check the winding for short circuits between wires and between the wiring and the laminations. I was fortunate to find someone who would perform this test on my rewinding job. I am happy to report that it passed. I did a quick dynamometer test using the Proto 3 inverter/controller, which I had used on the 1 hp motor. That test was promising as well. But, as before, the switching circuits failed with a battery voltage greater than 24 volts.

The Big Test at Ray Electric Outboards

During this period, I had discussed my project with Morton Ray. Mort is the owner of Ray Electric Outboards, Inc. of Cape Coral, Florida. He's a retired Signal Corp officer and a West Point graduate with an advanced degree in engineering. His company builds more electric outboards than anyone else in the world. As an engineer, Mort was also curious to know how well a 3 phase AC motor compared with the DC motors that he used.

We agreed to set up a test. Mort would furnish the DC motor and I would furnish the AC motor. He would modify the leg of one of his production outboards so that each one of the two motors could be belted to the outboard's drive shaft. The main idea was to run the outboard leg in a test tank with a stock propeller and measure the rpm of the outboard's drive shaft. We would then measure the voltage and the current drawn from the battery at various shaft speeds. From this data we would determine the input power required by each motor in order to obtain a given shaft speed.

In effect, the modified outboard leg would act as a dynamometer: as the shaft speed increased, the load would increase also. Obviously, the motor that required the least input power to obtain a given shaft speed would be the most efficient. By testing the efficiency of the motors in this manner, we felt the results would be beyond question.

For me, this would be a watershed event. I had decided that I would not pursue the 3 phase AC motor research if the results were not favorable.

Preparing for the Big Test

I had six weeks before returning to Florida. I wanted to build an inverter/controller capable of running at 48 volts and overcome the 24 volt limit that I had previously encountered.

At the time, I thought my problem was probably due to electrical noise in the logic caused by the switching action of the Mosfets switches. I decided to build a new control logic board, simplifying the logic as much as possible. For the time being, I would dispense with such niceties as the forward/reverse feature and the safety features. The Proto 5 logic board did not use the 33033 chip and operated the electronic switches with only six ICs (Integrated Circuits). I was able to run at a battery voltage up to 36 volts but the switches failed at 42 volts.

Last Minute Checkout

Time was now getting short. I decided to give it one more shot. For Proto 6, I would go back to using the 33033 chip and drive the electronic switches directly from the output of the 33033. The N channel Mosfets that I had been using were acceptable for the bottom switches, but I had to change to P channel Mosfets for the top switches. This basic controller had only four Ics. I hoped this controller would make it possible to operate the motor at full power. I ran it on the dynamometer, but I did not want to push it too hard, seeing that the safety circuits had not been implemented. At 36 volts, the efficiency was about 80%. I stopped right there and packed the motor and controller for the trip to Florida.

The Big Test

When I arrived at Mort's shop, I explained that very little checking had been done on this latest version of the inverter/controller. It was possible that we would not be able to run the experiment at the desired 48 volts. We agreed to start at 24 volts and go up in 6 volts increments to maximum power. The motor ran at 42 volts, something that I had never been able to get it to do before. Then the output switches not only blew up but caught on fire. An embarrassing end to the Big Test.

We had gathered enough data before the switch failure to determine that the 3 phase AC motor was about 10% more efficient than Mort's best DC motor. Later, Mort called to say he had plotted the results of the test and found that the efficiency of the AC motor was 14% better than the DC motor.

Results of the Big Test

The curves in Figure 9.1 show the results of the Big Test. To run the outboard at 1400 rpm, the DC motor required 900 watts vs. 700 watts for the AC motor. At 1600 rpm, the DC motor required 1350 watts vs. 1150 watts for the AC motor.

The curves also showed that as the power level increased, the difference between the two motors became less significant. This was consistent with our general understanding that the DC motors were most efficient at their rated power but the efficiency declined at less than full power, whereas the AC motors were as efficient at half power as they were at full power.

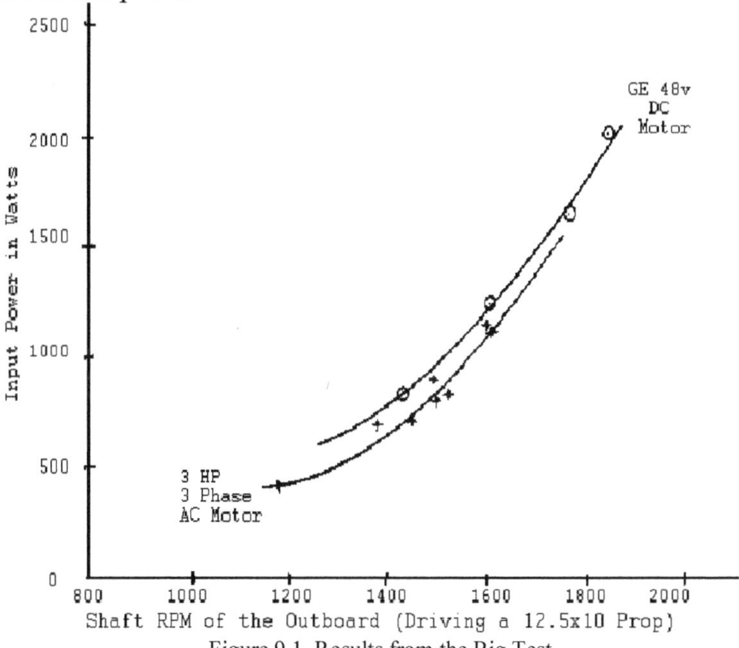

Figure 9.1 Results from the Big Test

No-load Tests

One reason for the lower efficiency of the DC motors is that they have to overcome the drag of the brushes on the commutator. To illustrate this difference, before leaving Mort's shop, we measured the "no load" power required to operate various motors at 2000 rpm without any attachments to the shaft. The box below shows the results of that test. The first two motors were the ones that Mort used on his production electric outboards. The third was our old friend the Baldor golf cart motor. The three AC motors are the 1 hp Lincoln, the 3 hp that was used in the Big Test and a 2 hp AC motor that I rewound a year or so after the test. I have also updated the chart by adding the no load power of the Etek motor.

No Load Test of Various Motors		
Motor Type	Current/Volts	Power
Mort, GE	5.1a at 36 v.	183 watts
Mort's # 2	5.3a at 48 v.	254 watts
Baldor	5.0a at 36 v.	180 watts
1HP AC	2.0a at 12 v.	24 watts
2HP AC	3.0 a at 12v.	36 watts
3HP AC	1.9 a at 36v.	68 watts
Etek	3.2 a at 24v.	77 watts

Clearly, the DC motors are very inefficient at no or low loads. They had to overcome a substantial internal load before being able to drive the external load attached to the shaft. The very efficient Etek permanent magnet motor shows results very similar to the AC motors.

I bought one of Mort's DC motors so that I could continue doing comparison tests between DC and AC motors on my dynamometer.

Repairing the Damage

Going from Proto 6, used in the Big Test, to Proto 10, my final design, was an arduous road. The main problem was finding out what caused the Mosfet switches to blow up when the battery voltage was raised to 48 volts. That turned out to be caused by the switching action of the Mosfets. It had nothing to do with the logic. That's why operating the logic from a printed circuit board (Proto 4) instead of the point to point wiring (Proto 3) did not show any improvement.

Destructive Glitch

The problem, it turned out, was caused by a large unwanted pulse that occurred when the Mosfet switches were turned **off.** This pulse got larger as the battery voltage and/or the current were increased. Most of the failures occurred at start-up because the starting current was four or five times larger than the running current.

To correct the problem, my first step was to obtain a Mosfet switch rated at 100 volts instead of the 55 and 60 volt Mosfets that I had been using. This additional safety factor between the Mosfet rated voltage and the battery voltage (the "head room") probably would have solved the problem by itself but additional protection devices were added as well.

One Mosfet instruction manual, which characterized this destructive pulse as "common, but easily corrected" proposed three methods of limiting the amplitude of these pulses. I tried them all, but only the "snubbers" which are designed to absorb the destructive energy of the pulse worked well for me. I settled on a very simple circuit using a 10 ohm resistor and a 1 microfarad capacitor. The trade-off here was between cutting the amplitude of the pulse and reducing the efficiency of the switching circuit.

More Development Work

Another area that needed work was the drive circuit for the Mosfet. Essentially, there was a trade off between complexity, speed and cost of the drive circuit that was not obvious at first. Motorola's Mosfet design notes showed thirteen different ways to drive the gate of the Mosfet. I tried a number of these and they all worked quite well.

I settled on the more expensive 2112 driver specifically designed for the job for three main reasons: first, it provided a valuable safety feature. Second, it provided a simple method of adjusting the switching speed of the Mosfet. This was important because there is a direct relation between switching speed and the size of the destructive pulse mentioned above. Third, having eight Mosfets in parallel required more gate driving power than some of the simpler drivers were capable of delivering.

Finally, I implemented the functions that had been previously checked out but placed on the back burner until some of the more critical circuits had been solidified. In Proto 7, the reverse and the anti-ambiguity circuits were restored. In Proto 9, the protection circuits, like over-current and under-voltage, were implemented. Proto 8 was another version of Proto 7 except that it was built on a printed circuit board, this time with a ground plane on one side of the board. Proto 10 was essentially the same as Proto 9 except for a repackaging job to make the inverter/controller fit in a metal enclosure.

Performance Results of the 3 hp Motor

The most important performance result was the ability to run successfully at 48 volts with a good margin of safety. During the experiments with snubbers, the 3 hp motor was connected in delta and started and stopped hundreds of times. The average starting current at 48 volts was 160 amps when the over-current protection was removed from the circuit. Considering that the operating current would be in the 40 amp range, I felt that I had a good margin of safety.

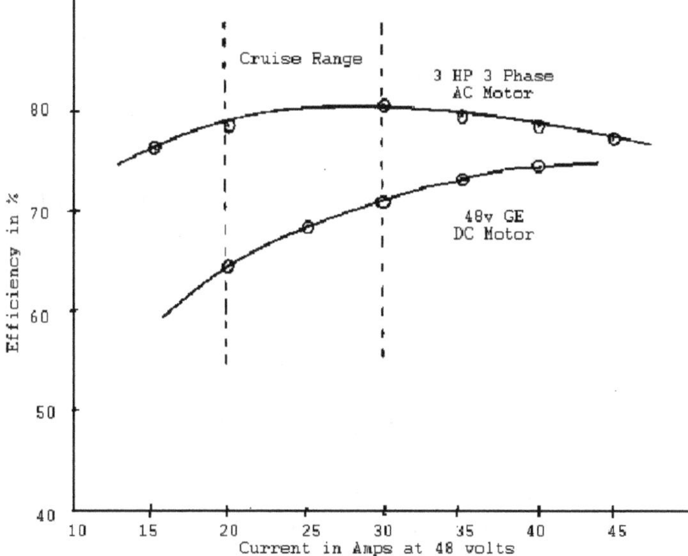

Figure 9.2 Efficiency Tests 3 hp AC Motor vs GE DC Motor

During these experiments, I found that the motor ran as efficiently connected in wye (one lead at each end of the letter Y) as in delta and that the wye starting current was less than half of the delta starting current. This important discovery would have saved me a lot of time and an untold number of Mosfet switches if I had made it earlier.

During the Big Test, we found out that the 3 phase AC motor is at least 10% more efficient than a comparable DC motor. Predictably, the AC motor was closer to the efficiency of the DC motor near its full power rating, but at half power or less, the efficiency advantage of the AC motor got increasingly better. The no-load tests also showed that the AC motor required far less power than the DC motor.

Using the latest version of the inverter/controller (Proto 10), the efficiency of the 3 hp AC motor was compared to that of the GE DC motor. These tests were done on my dynamometer. The curves in Figure 9.2 show the following results: the AC motor was more efficient by 15% at half power of 20 amps, 10% at 30 amps and 3% at full power of 45 amps.

Lessons Learned from the 3 hp Tests Using a 3 Phase AC Motor

We should think of these test results as a good first cut for both the inverter/controller and the new windings of the motor.

Regarding the inverter/controller, the drive circuits still needed to be optimized and more work could be done to reduce the noise pulses without affecting the efficiency of the switching circuits.

A computer controlled AC wave shape would likely improve the efficiency of the motor even more. This would be somewhat akin to what the electronic fuel control did to improve the efficiency of the automobile engine.

Regarding the new windings in the motor, fewer turns with heavier wire would also improve the efficiency. More copper in each slot is the key to high-efficiency motors. My best guess is that an overall improvement of 5% beyond what is shown on the curves is easily achievable.

I feel that the results shown here, tested in Mort's lab and on my dynamometer leave little doubt that the 3 phase AC motor is a fine candidate to power electric boats. The efficiency improvement of 10% over the best DC motor available was a good start but I did continue the work of improving the efficiency of the Inverter/controller with pulse width modulation and improve on the techniques for rewinding motors.

In the rest of this long chapter, I will show some of the interesting results of rewinding a 2 hp AC motor with two different sets of windings. I will also touch on the work done using a computer to control the output switches which generate the 3 phase AC power. This might get a little bit more technical than most readers will want to endure!

The 2 hp Three Phase AC Motor

In choosing the 2 hp motor that I planned to use on the Carolina Skiff, I emphasized the fact that it would be used as an electric outboard, a "kicker" in addition to the main power plant. The C face mounting and the light weight of the motor were important requirements. I also wanted to combine these features with a high efficiency motor. Unfortunately, I could not readily find one.

I settled for a 2 hp GE motor with a rated efficiency of 81.9% (not a premium efficiency motor) and a service factor of 115%, which meant that it could run continuously at 2.3 hp. The cost was $185.00 at W.W. Grainger.

Before unraveling the 230/460 volt windings, I did run it on the 3 phase inverter/controller that I was working on at the time. At 42 volts, it took 1 amp to operate at 2000 rpm. For the fun of it, I hooked it to an outboard motor leg and let the propeller blow a little wind. The propeller operated between 750 and 1100 rpm with a current drain of only 1.2 amps (50 watts).

Rewinding the 2 hp Motor

This last motor to be tested came with both a face plate mounting for an outboard configuration and a base plate which was handy for the dynamometer tests.

While unwinding the 230 volt winding from the new 2 hp motor, I found that it had been wound with 52 turns of #20 wire in each slot. I wanted to use the same 5 to 1 ratio that I had previously used (which would call for 10 turns), but I also wanted to determine the effect of a larger number of turns on the efficiency. I decided to try 12 turns per slot first, take a set of efficiency measurements and then rewind the motor with the 10 turns per slot.

The factory winding of 52 turns of #20 wire yielded a total area of 53,040 circular mils of copper in each slot. 12

turns of #14 wire produced an area of 49,320 circular mils. The second rewind used 10 turns of double #16 wire, which produced 51,600 circular mils. **For best efficiency, it is desirable to keep the coil resistance to a minimum by using the largest size of wire possible in each slot.**

An interesting aside is that the 3 hp motor, which was only 50% more powerful, had 102,000 circular mils of copper in each slot, which is almost twice as much copper as the 2 hp motor. No doubt that this had a lot to do with the high 90.2% efficiency rating of the 3 hp motor vs. the average 81.9% efficiency of the 2 hp motor.

Performance Results of the 2 hp Motor

The curves in Figure 9.3 show two things: one, the comparison between the 2 hp motor and the GE DC motor, and two, the comparison between the two versions of the 2 hp motor with two different windings.

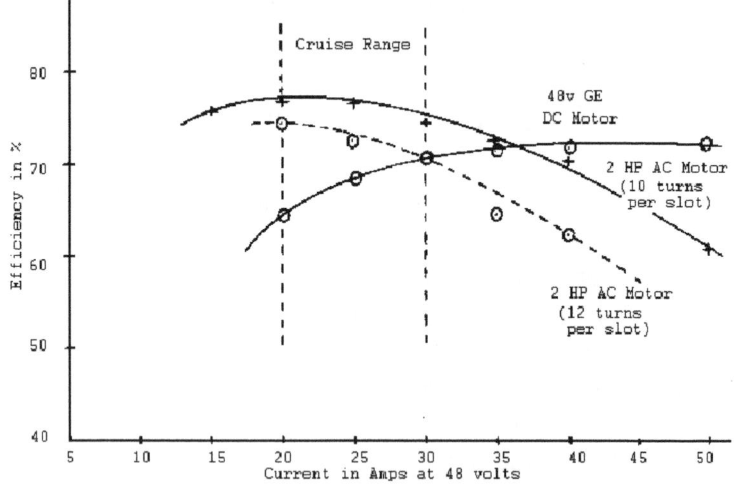

Figure 9.3 2 hp AC Motor (2 Different Windings) vs. GE DC Motor

Comparing the two windings of the 2 hp motor shows a significant improvement of the ten turn winding over the twelve turn winding. For the twelve turn per slot winding, I used a ratio of 4.3 to 1. The ratio of the rated voltage of 230 volts divided by the battery voltage of 48 volts is 4.8, so I knew that we would be on the low side. The 10 turns per slot winding had a ratio of 5.2 to 1 (52 factory wound turns divided by 10 turns). The improvement was most noticeable at the higher current of 40 amps (about 2000 watts), where the ten turn winding was 4% more efficient than the twelve turn winding.

From the analysis done at a later time, using the peak to peak voltage for the AC instead of the rms (root mean square) value (325 volts instead of 230 volts) the ratio should have been 6.7 instead of 5. If I were to rewind the motor again, I would try 8 turns of #12 wire. From my interpretation of the curves, that should be an even more efficient winding for this motor.

The comparison between the 3 phase AC motor and the GE DC motor shows that the two motors are approximately equal in efficiency at 40 amps, which is the full power output for the 2 hp motor. The comparison also shows the AC motor at 20 amps is 6% more efficient. Considering that neither the windings nor the electronics were completely optimized for this test, I feel that it is a good showing. We should also recall that this 2 hp AC motor is not of the premium efficiency category. Starting with a high efficiency motor would by itself improve the efficiency by 10% if we can use the 3 hp motor's performance as a guide.

Efficiency, Waste of Energy and a Better Battery Operated Motor

My fixation on efficiency is about not wasting energy. We have seen how the 2 hp and the 3 hp AC motors do the same job as the equivalent DC motor at a higher level of efficiency. This means that they waste less energy in the form of heat. Everyone is well aware that, except for solar power, there is a finite supply of energy and that conserving it is worthwhile effort. Even if we don't actually run out, the cost of energy is sure to increase as the supply decreases.

To be sure, even if all DC motors were replaced by AC motors, the impact on the planet's supply of energy would not be significant, but I believe that every little bit counts and that we should do what we can to help.

Photo 9.1 shows the far more complex armature of the DC motor vs. the simple AC rotor. The cost of the complex armature with its copper windings is obviously much greater and its maintenance costs are higher as well.

I would be remiss if I did not mention the superior safety aspect of the AC armature. It does not require brushes which cause sparking while carrying the substantial amount of current needed to generate the magnetic fields in the DC motors.

Photo 9.1 AC Rotor vs. DC Armature

A Hi-Tech Way to Improve the AC Motor's Efficiency

From the encouraging results obtained from the Big Test as well as the dynamometer testing, I felt it would be worthwhile to try out a few more ideas. I worked mainly on two of them. First, I modified the square wave to make it look more like the sine wave for which the AC motor is designed.

Second, it is known that a motor operating at less than full power should be supplied a lower voltage commensurate with the lower power requirement. A dramatic example of this rule can be seen when a motor is run at no load. The following data was obtained from experiments using the 3 hp AC motor while I was working on snubbers for the switching circuits.

At 12 volts, 2000 rpm, no load on the motor, the current was 1.8 amps or 21.6 watts.

At 36 volts, 2000 rpm, no load on the motor, the current was 1.9 amps or 68.4 watts.

Basically, the ampere turns do the work, irrespective of the voltage. More voltage than is needed merely creates more wasted heat, in this case three times as much!

How can these two efficiency enhancing ideas be implemented? Pulse width modulation (PWM), which we have already discussed, is the part of the answer the other part is to use a computer processor to control the operation of the motor. Let us review the PWM concept which may be a little difficult to understand.

Pulse Width Modulation

PWM devices which are used to control the speed of a DC motor generally run at a frequency of 15000 cycles per second. This frequency is selected primarily to be above the audio range so that its operation cannot be heard. A lower frequency might be annoying but would work equally well or perhaps a little better because high switching frequencies reduce the efficiency of the motor slightly.

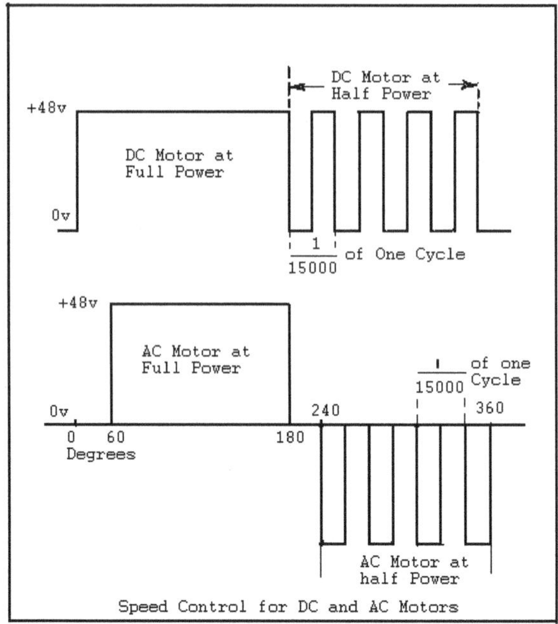

Speed Control for DC and AC Motors

The top half of the diagram shows that the DC motor will run at full power when the full width of the pulse is used. In the right hand side of the diagram, where each pulse is turned off (modulated) half of the time, the motor operates at half power. Similarly, in the bottom half of the diagram, if the AC motor were to operate with pulses half the width of the full power pulses, it would also operate at half power.

The square wave in the diagram has a time period of one cycle or one sixtieth of a second. If we were to show the PWM pulses at 15000 cycles per second (Hz), they would not be visible in the drawing, so only four such pulses are shown. When these half-on, half-off pulses are fed to the motor, it operates at half power. The reason is that the winding of the motor, being highly inductive, is not be able to react to the very high speed switching. Instead, the motor thinks that the voltage has been reduced by half. The electronics can be designed so that any amount of voltage reduction can take place from 0 to 99%.

Simulating an AC Sine Wave

Simulating an AC sine wave can be done with PWM or with a series of pulses (which is a lot easier to do with a computer). In the figure shown in the box below, a series of 20 pulses (#1 to #20) are shown. They make up a square wave that could be the positive half of phase A. But, notice that pulses 1, 2, 5, 15, 18 and 20 have been omitted. I averaged the value of the remaining pulses. The result was a wave that looks a lot more like a sine wave. With enough pulses during a time period, a close duplicate of the sine wave can be obtained. But we know that switching at too high a rate will cause the efficiency to deteriorate. The trick is to simulate the sine wave for maximum effect with a minimum number of pulses.

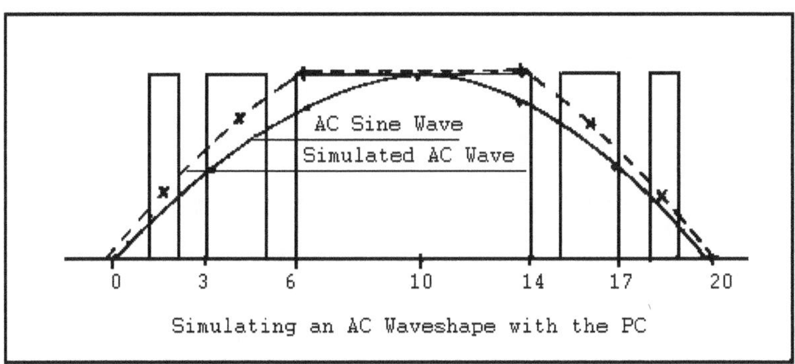

Simulating an AC Waveshape with the PC

Obviously, selecting a few pulses to be turned off out of a string of millions of pulses for each of 3 phases would require a very serious logic design effort. An easier way to solve this problem is to connect a microprocessor to the output switches and let the microprocessor control the operation of the six switches.

The Computer to the Rescue

Before actually designing a microprocessor hard wired version of the logic, it is wise to check the whole idea as well as the electronics and the software on a PC. With my son's help (he wrote the software), we connected a PC with a 386 microprocessor to the Mosfet power switches.

The computer output levels came out of the parallel printer port. A simple interface was built to convert the printer levels to match the inverter/controller logic levels. We kept the anti-ambiguity circuits in case a spurious pulse should happen to come through the interface. From the interface chips, the computer levels went to the switch drivers, which, in turn, activated the Mosfet output switches.

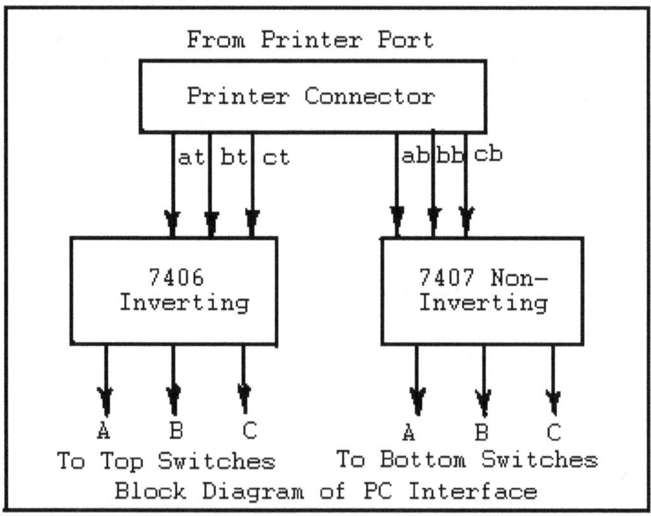

Block Diagram of PC Interface

Building the electronics was a very straightforward job. A block diagram of the interface is shown above. The diagram shows that the output from the PC comes out of the printer cable and works its way through the interface to the switch drivers and to the same Mosfet switches, which generate the 3 phase AC power for the motor.

The Computer Program

While building the hardware interface was simple enough, developing and writing the program was a far more complex endeavor. The software incorporated the main functions of the inverter/contoller, namely:

Generate the 3 phase AC wave shapes.

Control the speed of the motor with the frequency.

Start/stop the motor.

Reverse the rotation of the motor.

Many of the efficiency enhancing ideas were tried also. A diagram showing the computer generated pulses for phase A of the 3 phase AC motor is shown below. Full power and ¾ power are depicted.

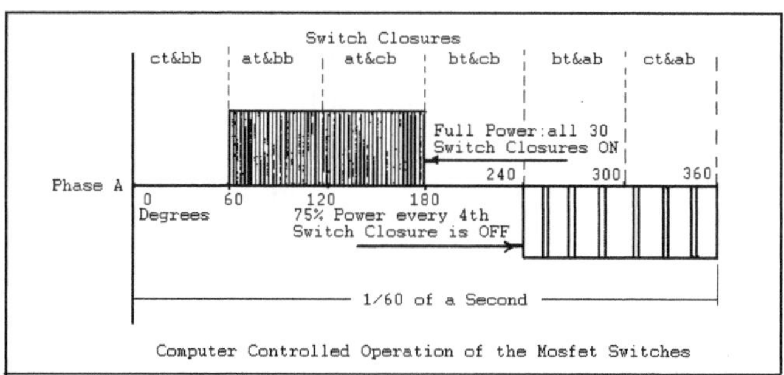

Computer Controlled Operation of the Mosfet Switches

With access to every one of the ninety switch closures in each AC cycle for each of the six switches, we had an opportunity to try a number of different ideas to improve the efficiency of the motor. We did not try them all by any means.

Computer Controlled Motor

The most important conclusion is that computer control of the Mosfet switches works very well. We divided the AC wave into 90 pulses (4 degree pulses) It turned out that the 386 microprocessor could have handled 180 pulses per wave (2 degree pulses) with ease.

Two degree pulses would surely have done a better job smoothing out the square wave into AC than 4 degree pulses. But I believe that the improvement in efficiency would have been minimal.

In hindsight, one feature that would have been worth incorporating in a computer controlled device was a method of reducing the in-rush of starting current to the motor. A simple timing routine would provide this feature.

Commercial Application for the Computer Control of a 3 Phase AC Motor

The electronics for a computer controlled 3 phase AC motor could be built into the motor as follows: the Mosfet switches could be built into the frame of the motor as are the diodes of alternators used in automotive applications. The rest of the logic, when optimized, could easily fit in a control box about the size of a cell phone. The on/off and speed control switches could be mounted in the junction box where the wires are interconnected in the present motors or operated remotely via a cable connection.

Future of the AC Motor in Boating

Is there any future hope for the 3 Phase AC motor in boating? I believe there is. New types of batteries are coming and they will replace the lead acid batteries. These batteries, either the Nickel Metal Hydrite (Ni-MH) or the Lithium ion (Li-ion) will be used in electric cars by the millions, consequently the prices will come down (more on the new batteries in Chapter 12). These batteries packs will be lighter (which is not a big help in a boating application) but they will also have a much higher voltage. The nickel hydride battery pack used in the Prius has an output voltage of 274 volts and many other hybrids also operate in the 300 volt range.

With the voltage at more than 230 volts, an off-the-shelf AC motor could be used since it would not have to be rewound. Moreover, the objection to the use of power transistors (you may remember that there is a voltage drop of 2 volts, which is wasted, at each switch position) is also obviated. Therefore, some of the 230/460 volt 3 phase inverters on the market could be used with a minor redesign.

It will take some time before we will know if any of the electric car components are a good fit for boating applications, but I believe that it will come to pass.

There is also a place for the three phase AC motor in boats larger than my four electric conversions beginning at 35 feet. For example, using a 240 volt battery packs made up of 20-12 volt deep cycle batteries operating at 35 amps, they would produce 8400 watts or 11 hp. High voltage configurations such as these could also use off-the-shelf AC motors and existing AC inverter/controller parts.

Lessons Learned in Chapter 9

Many lessons were learned from all this work but the most important one is that the 3 Phase AC motor is more efficient by at least 10% than the DC golf cart motors like the GE and the Baldor. This efficiency is equal to the Etek/Lynch permanent magnet motors.

We can also say that with just one moving part, the 3 phase AC is more reliable than any commutator based motor. And since it does not cause sparks and since the solenoids that normally start/stop and reverse the direction of the motor are not needed, they cannot cause sparks either making the motor safer for boating applications.

And all these advantages come at half the price!

Yet, today, the main components: a 48 volt AC motor and its inverter/controller are not a product that can be bought. The first edition of this book has been out for 8 years so the idea has been around for a while yet there has been no motion that I can discern towards such a product.

The next best boating motor is the Etek which, teamed with a good controller such as the Curtis, is an excellent power plant for an electric boat as was demonstrated with the Rhodes 19 conversion.

Concerning the work done with the 2 hp motor to improve efficiency, we can definitely show that the number of turns and the size of the wire greatly affect efficiency and must be optimized. We can also say that the computer controlled switching is the proper method of tweaking the efficiency further. Although I did not come up with the best formula to optimize the efficiency, I can say with certainty that better results can be obtained with more work in this area.

My main problem was the lack of resources to rewind several identical motors (3 or 4) with a variety of number of turns and size of wire. Then, when using the software to say, smooth out the square wave, the efficiency of different motors could have been tested. There is an interaction between wave smoothing and the number of turns (because wave smoothing reduces the voltage) that cannot be evaluated with a single motor.

So, I leave these interesting experiments to someone else. It would not be fair for me to have all the fun!

CHAPTER 10

Boat Hulls

In the next three chapters, we explore the theory behind the results obtained with the four electric boat conversions. We know that to obtain good cruising speed and range, given the limited amount of energy that can be stored in batteries, the design of the hull, the size and speed of the propeller, the efficiency of the motor and the size of the battery pack must all be optimized.

But, in all these areas, perfection is not attainable at a reasonable price. A long, narrow boat is easy to power but it is not stable enough for safe and comfortable boating. A large, slow turning prop is most efficient but it needs reduction gears and the limited space under the hull of smaller boats does not permit its installation. Most of the available DC electric motors are designed for other applications and do not generate their optimum efficiency at the boat's cruising speed.

These are the trade-offs that face an electric boater. In these next three chapters we examine the theory behind these necessary trade-offs and attempt to provide practical guidelines to make the best of them.

Today's Popular Cruising Boats

Today's most popular boat in the 18 to 22 ft range is a runabout with a deep V hull. It is likely to be powered by an inboard/outboard engine or a large outboard or even twin outboards. At cruising speed, it will plane at more than 30 mph and operate fairly comfortably in 3 ft seas found offshore.

Such a boat requires an enormous amount of power. A pair of 150 hp outboards are often recommended. These boats are used mostly for fishing offshore or pleasure cruises outside of the harbor.

Photo 10.1 Indian Canoe, Sitka, Alaska

It was not always so. At the turn of the 20th century, when internal combustion engines were first installed in boats, great care was taken to design an efficient hull that could be propelled at hull speed with a power plant in the order of 2 hp.

Long before that, the Alaskan Indians built long, narrow fishing boats that were powered by paddles. Photo 10.1, taken in Sitka, Alaska, next to the library, shows a reproduction of a 50 ft Indian canoe. This boat was called the "everybody" canoe. The description does not reveal whether it took the whole village to carve it out or whether it could take the entire village for a boat ride.

I'm not recommending that we go back to the old days in order to enjoy boating. For those who like speed or need a speedy run to the fishing grounds, today's boats are perfect. But many other boaters like a more leisurely and quiet boat excursion. Most of the interesting scenery is near shore not in the middle of the ocean. Personally, I find cruising in a bay or a lake far more pleasant than having to hang on for dear life under adverse conditions in the middle of nowhere. For some of us, electric cruising is ideal.

Hull Speed

Boat hulls are designed to be either planing hulls or displacement hulls. The planing boats are the "go fast" boats capable of reaching 30 or more mph while providing a fairly comfortable ride in a choppy sea. They usually have deep V hulls and very powerful engines. They are not candidates for electric power because it is not possible to store a sufficient amount of energy in batteries. To store the amount of energy available in fifty gallons of gas (which a deep V hull would gobble up in a couple of hours) would require 17,500 lbs of batteries--enough to sink the boat.

Displacement hulls, on the other hand, go much slower but require far less energy to drive the boat. All displacement hulls are not necessarily easy to drive but a well designed hull that you might find in a sailboat, will provide the best speed for a given amount of power.

The maximum speed of a displacement hull, usually referred to as "the hull speed," is calculated as the square root of the waterline dimension of the boat multiplied by the constant 1.34. A sailboat (like *Sunny)* 23 feet in length with a 19 ft waterline would have a hull speed of 4.35 x 1.34 or 5.75 knots. One knot is equal to 1.15 mph, so the hull speed of this sailboat would be 6.6 mph.

This formula determines the most efficient maximum speed of a properly designed displacement hull. It is not a magical number that can't be exceeded. The boat will not slow down if a little more power is applied. But exceeding hull speed takes much more **incremental power** to obtain a small increase in speed. Eventually, if enough power is applied to a displacement hull, the boat will squat in the water, make bigger waves and eventually it will indeed slow down.

The only practical way to increase the speed of a boat with a displacement hull is to increase the length of the waterline. That becomes expensive very quickly when you consider that a boat with a 64 ft waterline has a hull speed of 8 x 1.34 or 10.5 knots, less than double the hull speed of the boat with the 19 ft waterline, yet it costs twenty times as much.

Hull Designs for Electrically Powered Boats

The most efficient hull that I have seen is a 19 ft, one man, sea-going kayak weighing 32 lbs. The owner told me that he traveled at 7 mph continuously using a double-ended paddle. When you consider that he was generating, at most, one tenth of one horsepower, that was quite a feat. Sculls, with their extreme length to beam ratios, also attain amazing speeds with six or eight rowers who generate approximately one horsepower.

These extreme designs are not suitable for pleasure cruising. The beam of the boat needs to be much wider to make it stable, but a wider beam will increase the power requirement. The electric boats on the market today, such as the Duffy 18, Mort Ray's Explorer and the Elco's, have beam measurements of about 6 feet for a boat approximately 20 feet in length. These "picnic boats" are perfect for day cruising.

Mort's Boats

Another way to obtain good speed with a minimum amount of power is to follow Mort Ray's lead in the development of a catamaran with long narrow super-efficient hulls. His extremely roomy 26 ft "Electrocat" is capable of achieving 5.5 mph with a power drain of only 25 amps at 48 volts (1.6 hp). This is quite an achievement for a vessel weighing 3600 lbs.

Mort was good enough to provide me with some actual data of the operation of his boats as shown in the Figure 10.1.

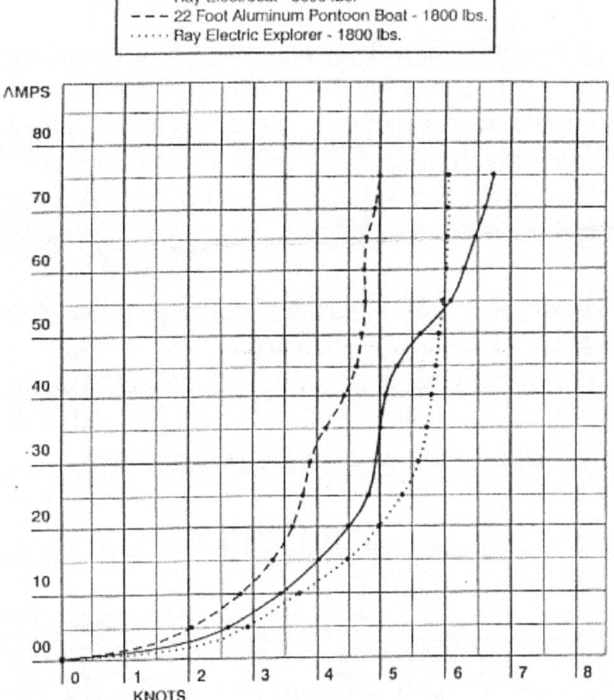

Figure 10.1 Ray Electric Boats Performance Graphs
(Courtesy of Ray Electric Outboards)

The Ray Explorer

At a battery current of 30 amps (1440 watts at 48 volts), we find that the 21 ft Ray Explorer travels at 5.6 knots. With a waterline measurement of approximately 19 feet, the theoretical hull speed is 1.34 X square root of 19 or 5.8 knots. Notice that to increase the speed from 5.6 knots to 6.0 knots, the battery current has to double from 30 amps to 60 amps. That's very good evidence that the "hull speed" formula really works.

The Ray Electrocat

The Electrocat curve shows an interesting knee formation, indicating that there are two efficient hull speeds, one at a lower speed than the other. The first one occurs at 4.9 knots (5.6 mph) with a battery drain of 30 amps. This is the most efficient operating speed. It is 1.1 knots (1.3 mph) faster than a 22 ft pontoon boat with the standard circular aluminum pontoons weighing far less, as is shown on the third curve.

After that point, due to the waves produced by the adjacent pontoons, it takes considerably more power to attain a higher speed. But unlike the single hull boats, once the interfering wave making is overcome, the Electrocat starts to gain momentum again and is able to reach a speed of 8 mph with approximately 3600 watts or 5 hp of input power.

All this Drag

So far, we've established two principles. Electric power is not compatible with planing hulls and to obtain a reasonable range at the best possible speed, the displacement hull must have the lowest possible water resistance or drag.

The drag that the electric motor has to overcome to

push the boat forward comes from two sources: the surface drag and the drag caused by wave-making. The general consensus is that one third of the total drag is from surface drag and two thirds is from wave-making. Since electrically powered boats operate at low speeds, where the wave-making is minimal, the surface drag is even more important. We will examine both types of drag in the following sections.

Surface Drag

Obviously, a hull full of barnacles and sea grasses is going to be much more difficult to drive than a clean one. A study made by Johnson Outboards showed that a boat left unused for forty days without cleaning the bottom, caused its speed to be reduced from 25 mph to 13 mph due to the accumulation of marine growth. We will assume that the owner keeps his boat clean and uses good quality bottom paint if the boat is left in the water for extended periods of time.

From a design standpoint, we will look at the cross section of the hull to see which type provides the minimum amount of surface for a given displacement. We will determine the amount of "wetted surface" that three different hull shapes with approximately the same displacement create. Less surface equates to less surface drag.

The 3 Hull Shapes

The three hull shapes that we will consider are the flat bottom, the deep V bottom and the round bottom hulls. The three simplified diagrams below show three hulls of radically different shapes with approximately the same displacement. The surface area is calculated for each hull shape.

The Flat Bottomed Hull

The flat bottom hull shown below has a beam of 7 feet with a length of 20 feet and a draft of 18 inches. The displacement of this hull shape is 20 x 7 x 1.5 ft or 210 cubic feet. Since water weighs 62.4 lbs per cubic ft, the displacement is 13,104 lbs. The total wetted surface is 20 x 7 feet for the bottom plus 54 x 1.5 for the sides, front and back or 221 square feet.

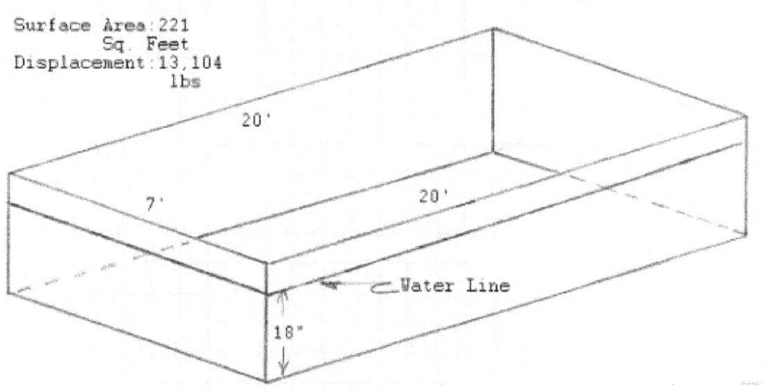

The Deep V Hull

The next shape to consider is the deep V shown in the diagram on the next page. The displacement of this hull shape is also 13,104 lbs. The wetted surface is 4.6 feet x 20 for each side or 184 square feet plus 21 square feet for the front and the back for a total of 205 square feet.

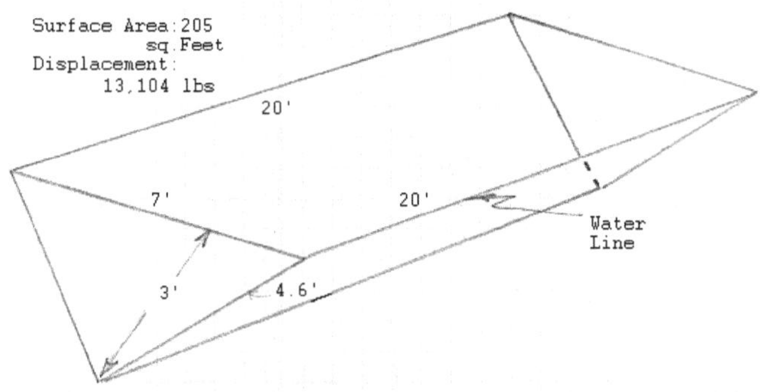

The Round Bottom Hull

The round bottomed hull shown in the diagram below has a beam of 61 inches instead of the 7 feet used above in order to displace approximately the same amount of water as the other two hulls of the same length. The diagram below shows the dimensions used to determine the displacement and the wetted surface. The displacement for a hull of this shape and size is 13,076 lbs and the surface area is equal to 183 square feet.

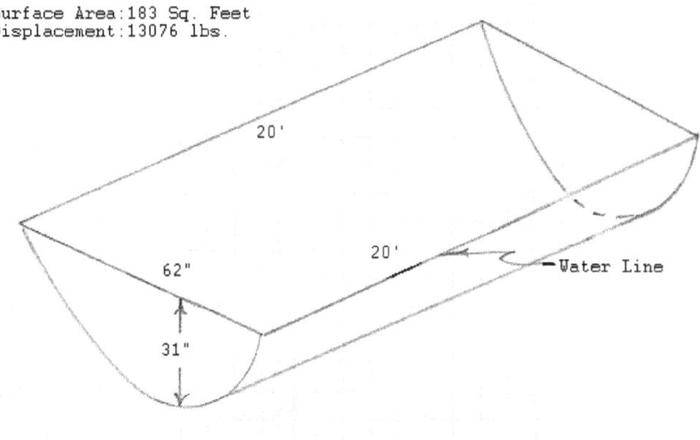

As we can see from the results, the round bottom boat easily wins this contest. It has about 10% less surface area than the deep V boat. The deep V hull has approximately 10% less surface area than the flat-bottomed boat.

These results surprised me. When I bought the Carolina Skiff, I naturally assumed that since it had an efficient hull for planing at low power, it would also operate efficiently in the displacement mode. When it comes to the resistance caused by the surface drag, the flat bottom hull comes in last. The best hull shape is the one used by most sailboats--an oval shaped bottom. It is only 10% better than the deep V hull, but when the boat power comes from batteries every little bit of efficiency helps.

Wave-making Drag

Although it varies with speed, the hull resistance caused by the wave-making action of the hull is generally deemed to be twice as important as the drag caused by the surface resistance. Although the subject of hydrodynamics is beyond the scope of this book, there are a few practical considerations worth highlighting.

The weight of the boat and the equipment on board contribute to both the wetted surface drag and the amount of water displaced, which in turn generate the power-robbing waves. Needless to say the weight should be kept to a minimum. The distribution of the weight is also important. In displacement hulls, better results can often be obtained by moving some of the weight forward. While I was doing in-the-water tests, I experienced as much as 1/2 knot improvement in speed simply by moving a couple of passengers forward to better balance the boat.

To minimize the effect of wave-making, the most important consideration is the longitudinal shape of the hull (not the cross-sections that we discussed previously). At the bow, the entry should be sharp or slanted to ride over the waves such as is done in the Boston Whaler and the Carolina Skiff.

The bow has other functions, such as providing a platform for fishing. It is generally flared to deflect the water and the spray to keep the boat reasonably dry. These features may reduce the bow's ability to cut through the water efficiently and increase the hull's drag.

Low Resistance Hulls

I have read everything that I could find on the subject of low resistance hulls. There isn't any great interest in the subject anymore as far as motorboats are concerned. Most of the writings are about boats that were popular 100 years ago when internal combustion engines for boats generated all of 2 horsepower. The hull designs are perfectly sound and can still be used to our advantage today.

We've already discussed two of the characteristics: long and slim lines with a length to beam ratio greater than 3 to 1 and an oval hull rather than a flat or a deep V hull. Two other characteristics repeated over and over are the shape of the bottom from the mid section to the stern, known as the rake, and the height of the transom.

Design of the Midsection of the Boat

The sketch below is a composite of hull shapes found in today's sailboats and also used in the low resistance boats of old. The angle between the waterline and the rising section of the hull, called the rake angle, distinguishes the displacement hull from a planing hull. An angle of approximately 10 degrees or more would be a displacement hull while an angle of 2 degrees or less would be a planing hull. The 5 or 6 degree rake, in the no-man's land between the two, is reserved for the semi-displacement hulls.

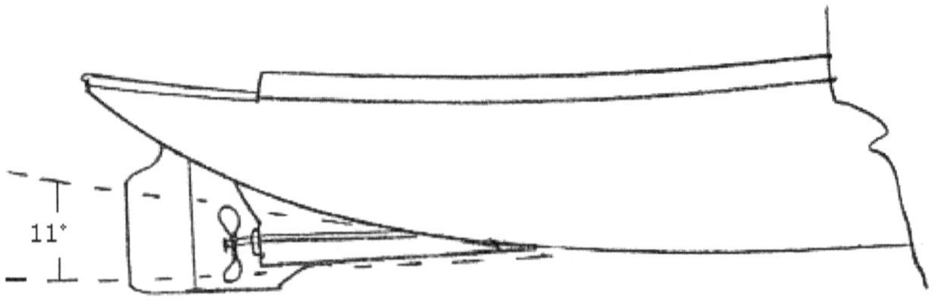

Sailboat with a Rake Angle of 11 degrees

A direct result of the angle discussed above is the height of the transom. If the rear portion of the hull is flat, as it would be for a planing hull, the bottom of the transom will be below the waterline. A rake angle of 10 degrees or more will cause the bottom of the transom to be above the waterline. When a planing hull is operated in displacement mode (running at a slow speed), a great deal of drag is created by the combination of the flat bottom and the turbulence behind the transom of the boat.

Mort Ray, president of Ray Electric Outboards, tells us in his brochure that he had an opportunity to perform some quantitative tests on a 16 ft Carolina Skiff with and without rake. To produce rake, he cut 9 inches from the bottom of the 20-inch transom, then went 36 inches forward of the transom and curved the bottom to meet back at the transom. These tests, he tells us, were used to determine "Ray's Rule of Rake," which says rake reduces the power required to produce displacement speeds by half.

Comparing Two Hull Types Displacement Hulls

Figure 10.2 compares the in-the-water tests of the four boats in Part 1. The first point to be made is the 23 ft *Sunny*, although 3 feet longer and at 1000 lbs heavier than the 20 ft

O'Day, required only 100 watts more power at speeds of 4 to 6 mph. The second point is that both sailboats attain hull speed with approximately 2000 watts of input power. The third point is that the Rhodes 19 is without peers in these tests. In fact, at 5.9 knots using 1400 watts, it matches the Ray Explorer.

From the curves, we can see that a very efficient cruising speed for *Sunny* would be 5.5 mph. At this speed, the battery drain would be approximately 30 amps from a 48 volt power pack. With a battery pack of eight, 6 volt golf cart batteries with a capacity of 220 ampere-hours, this level of current drain translates into a range of at least six hours and 33 miles. The Rhodes 19 uses far less power at this speed but since there are only three 12 volt batteries, the range would be about the same.

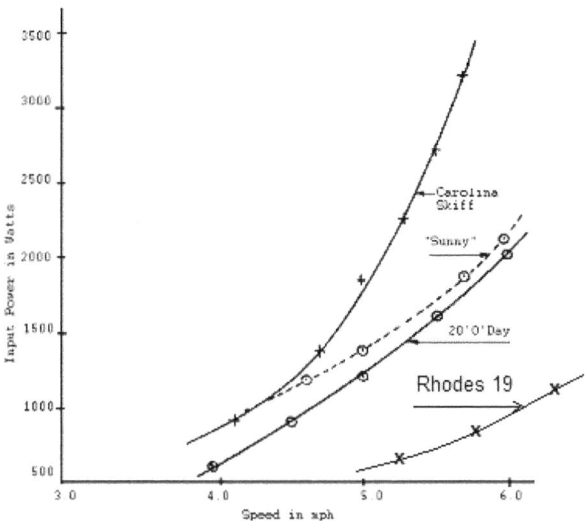

Figure 10.2 Performance of Four Electrically Powered Boats

Planing Hull

The 21 ft Carolina Skiff is also shown operating in displacement mode. It weighed only half as much as the two sailboats. But because it has a flat bottom and lacked sufficient rake, it required far more power than the sailboats. At 5.6

mph, which is a good cruising speed for the sailboats, it required about twice as much power. To obtain a reasonable range, the speed should be reduced to approximately 5 mph. In this case, the range with the eight six volt battery pack would be about five hours and 25 miles.

Putting the Theory to Good Use Primary or Auxiliary Source of Power

At this point, we will attempt to put some of this theory to the practical use of selecting an electric boat. We must assess whether the electric power will be used as the primary source of power for the boat or if it is to be used as an auxiliary source. As an auxiliary, the performance of the electric motor is not nearly as critical. Even at less than optimum efficiency, an electric drive will power any type of hull in the displacement mode.

The Electric Auxiliary

As an auxiliary source of power, for example, a "kicker" for a boat used mainly for fishing. Its main function is to troll or get back home in case of the failure of the main power plant. The main decision is to settle on the range, which is then used to determine the size of the battery pack.

Much the same can be said for the use of electric power as an auxiliary in a sailboat. An estimate should be made of the amount of running time that the electric power will be used to travel to the sailing area, set the sails and return to homeport in case the wind dies. A battery pack providing adequate running time can then be selected.

Primary Power

In the case where the electric drive is used as the primary power source, the decision is more difficult. If a new boat is going to be purchased, the choice is between the available candidates. The main attributes of the boat should be range, speed and the method of recharging the batteries. The specifications of the boat will certainly provide that information.

Converting a Used Boat to Electric Power

If a used boat is to be converted to an electric, as I did with *Sunny* and *Sunny II*, then much greater caution is advised. The main problem is to determine if the hull can be classified as a low resistance hull. To summarize the main characteristics:

Long and narrow shape
Elliptical cross section
Ample rake to keep the transom out of the water
Light weight

We have seen that most of these features are generally available in sailboat hulls. In spite of the computer designed boats and the tank testing that is usually done, the whole design process is still more art than engineering and it's easy to end up with a dud. It is best to select a design that has been around for a long time and has withstood the test of thousands of sailors. Good choices are the O'Day Rhodes 19 or a 22 ft Catalina or the J 24, which is said to be very slippery in spite of its generous beam.

Even with a set of boat drawings showing the sectional and the longitudinal lines of the boat, it is not easy to establish how well it will perform at low power. Boat designers claim to be able to "read" these drawings (meaning that they can visualize the operation of the boat from the drawing), but, for the rest of us mere mortals, these intricate designs do not reveal much beyond the length and the beam of the boat.

Drag Test

If it can be done before actually purchasing the hull, a more scientific way to determine whether the boat has a low resistance hull is to pull it in the water and measure the pulling force required.

With a tow boat pulling the boat to be tested, the pulling force is measured in lbs on good spring scales at various speeds such as 4, 5 and 6 mph. (The tow boat must be kept well ahead so that its wake will not affect the readings). By applying the formula: watts = Speed x Force, the output power of the motor, which propels the boat can be calculated at various speeds.

Drag of Sailboats

To determine the input power, which, in turn, determines the all-important drain from the battery, the output power must be divided by the combined efficiency of the motor and the propeller. For example if 60 lbs of force were required to pull the test boat at 5 mph, the power in watts is determined as follows: We know that 1 hp is equivalent to 550 ft-lbs per second. 5 mph is equal to 7.33 feet /second, so 60 x7.33 / 550 = 0.8 hp. To make the answer come out in watts, we multiply the hp by 746, or 597 watts. Assuming an excellent overall efficiency of 50% for the motor and the propeller, the input power drained from the battery pack would be 1194 watts or 1.6 hp.

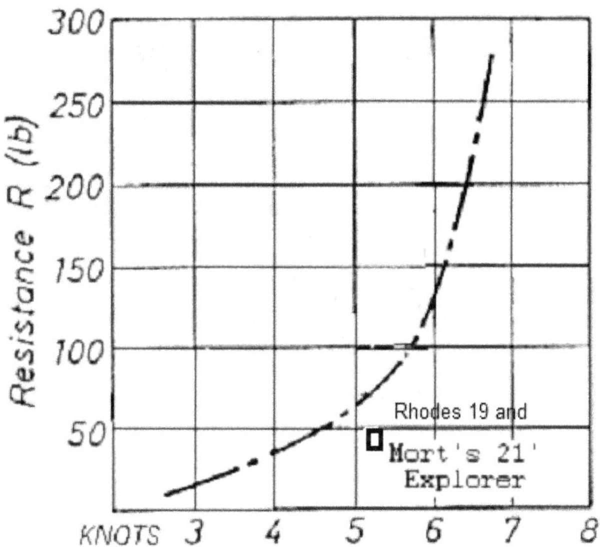

Figure 10.3 Hull Resistance of Sailboats

Figure 10.3 provides good average values of hull resistance (drag) at various speeds for sailboats of the size described here. At 5 knots, for example, an average sailboat has a resistance of 70 lbs.

The square on the graph shows the 48 lb resistance for the very low resistance hull of Morton Ray's 21 ft Explorer motoring at 6 mph. Unfortunately, I did not appreciate the value of this test when I owned the first three boats that we have been discussing. Consequently, I have no drag data for them.

My next electric boat, "*Sunny* II" was an O'Day Rhodes 19. I did not perform drag tests on this boat either but since it attained the same speed as Mort's with the same input power, we can assume that it has approximately the same drag.

Conclusions

1. A low resistance hull is vitally important for electric propulsion

2. Sailboats, because they are designed to operate from sails, which do not provide much power, generally have good low resistance hulls even with their generous beam.

3. To get a good idea of the performance that can be expected from an electrically driven boat, a drag test before buying the boat is a smart move.

CHAPTER 11

Propellers

Introduction

The propeller is also known in nautical circles as the prop, the screw and the wheel. The prop's function is to transform the rotating power of the motor into the forward thrust that moves the boat.

Unlike the automobile, where most of the rotating power from the motor is transformed into forward thrust with little loss, the prop wastes about half of the power that is transmitted to it. Making sure that as much power as possible is converted to forward thrust is essential in electrically powered boats. The following subjects are discussed in this chapter:

Determining the diameter of the propeller
Determining the pitch of the propeller
Selecting an efficient propeller using simple formulas and ratios

How Does the Propeller Work?

There is a mistaken impression that the prop somehow screws its way into a wall of water thereby pushing or pulling the boat forward. Actually, the forward thrust is the reaction from the massive jet of water, which is directed to the rear of the boat. It is somewhat like a fire-hose that requires two firemen to hold it as it tries to whip back and forth.

Propeller Characteristics

The single most important characteristic of the prop is its diameter. As a general rule, for a given application, the larger the prop, the more efficient it will be. There are limits. Bigger props cost more, weigh more and require more room under the boat. There is a propeller application rule claiming that the propeller efficiency will continue to improve until the prop reaches a size equal to one third of the beam of the boat at the waterline.

This rule may apply to very narrow boats but would obviously not work for a boat such as *Sunny or Sunny II.* According to that rule, *Sunny*, with a 7 ft beam at the waterline should have been fitted with a 28 inch prop to optimize its efficiency. A stock propeller of that size would cost over $1000 weigh more than 100 lbs and require a 2.5 inch shaft to drive it. Such a prop is designed to be driven by a 300 hp diesel not a 2 hp electric motor. This is an obvious overkill.

A Pictorial of the Situation

The sketch on the next page shows what increasing the 12 inch prop to 28 inches would do to the propeller installation on *Sunny*. The shaft angle would increase dramatically from 6 degrees to 15 degrees to accommodate the greater diameter of the larger prop and the additional clearance required (4 inches instead of 2 inches). Increasing the shaft angle would reduce the forward thrust because a greater portion of the input power would be wasted, serving only to push the stern in the upward direction instead of pushing the boat forward. The efficiency would suffer far more than could possibly be gained from a propeller that large. So much for "the third of the beam dimension" rule.

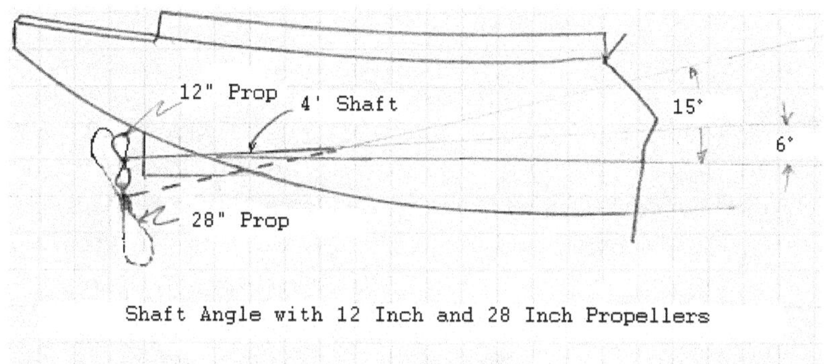

Shaft Angle with 12 Inch and 28 Inch Propellers

Efficiency of the Propeller

Before describing the formulas and charts used to determine the optimum size and pitch of a propeller, there are four considerations affecting the efficiency of the prop worth reviewing: the number of blades, the material and the size and speed of the prop.

The Number of Blades

For our purposes, a single-blade prop would be best. It is the most efficient because the blade encounters the least amount of water disturbance as it rotates. But, single-blade props are not available because they generate too much vibration. The two-blade prop is said to be about 2% more efficient than the three-blade prop and is perfectly acceptable. A three-blade prop is smoother and is acceptable also. Personally, I have never detected any difference between a two and a three-blade prop. A four-blade prop is needed only when space is at premium below the boat and the larger blade area is required to handle the power of the engine. It is not a good choice for electric power.

The Material

The material that the propeller is made of is the second consideration. Even though our horsepower requirements are minimal, the prop still needs to be rugged enough not to change its shape as it displaces the water. On the other hand, a thinner blade will offer the least resistance to the swirling water. Of the four materials generally used in propellers -- stainless steel, brass/bronze, aluminum, and plastic -- the stainless steel props are the most efficient. The blades are strong yet very thin. They are also the most expensive. The other three become less efficient in the order listed: brass/bronze, aluminum and plastic. However, some of the new composition plastics are made into very good, inexpensive propellers.

The Size and Speed of the Propeller

The third consideration is the size and speed of the prop. Figure 11.1, which I have partially copied from Lindsay Lord's article "Figuring your Prop," shows the amount of power required to rotate a prop without pitch, just blades going around that produce no forward thrust as they rotate. It shows that at 800 rpm, a 15 inch prop requires 1 hp while a 20 inch prop requires 4 hp. Obviously, the use of propellers that large would overwhelm a 2 hp electric power source.

The efficient prop that we are looking for should therefore have the minimum blade area capable of handling the power developed at the required rpm and should have the thinnest blades possible for minimum friction.

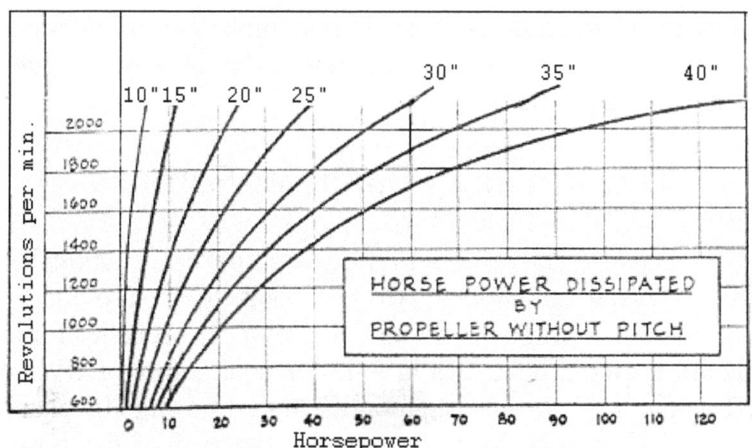

Figure 11.1 Power Dissipated by a Propeller without Pitch

Propeller Diameter for Electric Boats

We will discuss several methods of determining the size of the propeller depending on the size and type of boat, size of the motor and speed of the boat.

In all the literature I've read on electric boats trying to gain some knowledge from the experience of others, the largest prop I've seen recommended for an electric outboard was 15 inches in diameter. It was an experimental composition plastic prop with removable blades (which sounded like a good idea, but it was unavailable for sale). The stock propeller for that motor was 14 inches in diameter.

Of the many inboard electric boat designs, six are shown in Douglas Little's *Electric Boat Handbook.* The largest prop listed was 20 inches in diameter with a 30 inch pitch and a 10 to 1 reduction ratio--not your run of the mill design! The rest were 15 inches in diameter or less.

There is a good scientific way to pick the correct prop for an electric boat, but it is not easy or straightforward. One big problem is that the charts and formulas do not generally show data down to the 2 hp power range. The second problem is that the charts and formulas do not emphasize efficiency as a primary goal. We'll look at a few different ways to get a handle on the problem.

The Minimum Diameter Formula

David Gerr wrote an entire book on propellers called *The Propeller Handbook.* In his book, Gerr provided a formula to determine the minimum size of the propeller for an inboard powered boat: D min = 4.07 x square root of BWL x HD where BWL equals beam on the waterline and HD equals draft. The formula does not consider the size of the power plant, only the size of the boat.

For *Sunny*, this formula yields the following result: 4.07 x 2.64 x 1.22 = 13.1 inches. Since this is a formula to determine the minimum diameter, the first question is whether the size is sufficient to handle the motor power. Obviously, a 13 inch prop can handle the power output of 2 hp motor with ease. The second question is whether this is the most efficient size for the required prop. The answer is, probably not. If a slightly larger prop can be accommodated easily, it may be a better choice. At least we know that a 13 inch prop is a reasonable candidate for this boat.

Propeller Charts to Determine the Diameter of the Prop

Weston Farmer, in his book *From My Old Boat Shop* and Robert Kress and E.L. Lorenz of Michigan Wheel Co., in their article "Marine Propeller Selection" provide very easy-to-use charts for selecting the correct size of propeller. I've redrawn part of the chart in Figure 11.2.

One problem with using published formulas and charts to determine the size of the prop is they are designed to be used with far more powerful engines. Generally, the 2 or 3 hp available from the electric motor ends up being off the chart.

In the drawing below, I added a few lines so that the chart could be used for an electric application.

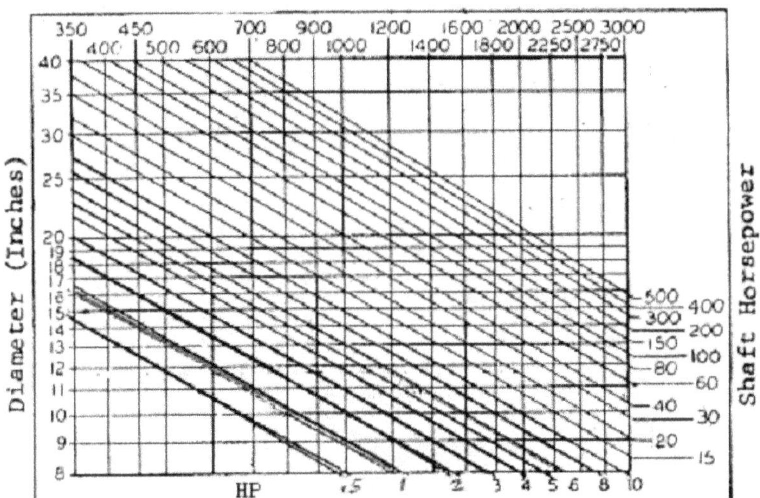

Figure 11.2 Selecting a Propeller

All that's needed is the hp of the motor and the rpm of the shaft. In the case of electric propulsion, the 3 hp line can be used. If the reduction gear reduces the speed to 1000 rpm, an 11 inch prop is needed. If the reduction gear provides a speed of 800 rpm, then a 12.5 inch prop is needed. It is very interesting to see how well these curves agree with results obtained from David Gerr's formula.

We don't know yet whether a prop with this diameter is the most efficient or whether it will yield a good propeller pitch for the appropriate boat speed. However, it is certainly a good starting point.

Propeller Pitch

The other important characteristic of the propeller is the pitch. If we were to consider the prop as a screw that twists its way into the water, it would move forward by the amount of the pitch of the prop. A propeller with a pitch of 10 inches would move forward by 10 inches for each revolution.

Propeller Slip and P/D Ratio		
Type of Boat	Slip	P/D
Michigan Wheel Co.		
Sailing Auxiliary	35/40%	.6/.7
Displacement Cruiser	30/40%	.8/1.0
Gerr's Handbook		
Sailing Auxiliary	45%	.6/.85
Work Boats	26%	.7/.9

As we pointed out, this is not the way it works in the real world. It is the reaction from the stream of water displaced by the prop that moves the boat forward. This forward movement in the example above is less than 10 inches per revolution. The actual amount of movement is 10 inches less the slip. The slip is generally referred to as a percentage. With a slip of 40%, the forward movement of the boat would be 10 inches less 40% of 10 or 6 inches for each revolution of the propeller. The chart above from Gerr's book and the Michigan Wheel Co. article shows a number of examples of the slip expected for different types of boats. The average slip for all the boats shown is 36%.

The 40% slip number used in the example above is reasonable for an auxiliary motor on a sailboat. To calculate the speed of the boat if the propeller pitch were 10 inches and the prop speed were 1000 rpm, we simply multiply 1000 times the pitch less the slip and arrive at a speed of 500 feet per minute, which equals 30,000 feet per hour or 5.7 mph.

Pitch to Diameter Ratio

The second column in the chart on the previous page shows the pitch to diameter ratio (P/D ratio) that is considered optimum for various boats. It is important to select the proper P/D ratio because it affects the efficiency of the drive. By putting both of these pieces of information together we can obtain a complete answer to the propeller selection process.

The chart showing the P/D ratio includes the information provided by both Gerr and the Michigan Wheel Co. article. We should try to use the high end of these values because the propeller efficiency improves as the pitch to diameter ratio increases. Assuming a 12 inch prop diameter with a 10 inch pitch, we obtain a P/D ratio of 0.83. The average of the four P/D ratios shown in the chart is 0.78.

A reassuring aside for this propeller selection process, is that the Ray Electric Outboard Co. uses a 12.5 inch x 10 inch pitch propeller for all their electric outboards. Mort Ray designed this prop specifically for a 3 hp motor running at approximately 3000 rpm with a 2.5 to 1 reduction ratio.

If a Ray outboard were installed on *Sunny* and we calculated the speed with a 40% slip, we would obtain the following results: 6 inches (.5 feet) forward movement for each revolution of the prop. Multiplying .5 ft by 3000 rpm divided by the 2.5 ratio, we obtain 600 feet per minute or 6.8 mph. This is within the ballpark of the results that I've obtained.

Blade Area

The Michigan Wheel Co. article provides the following formula for blade area: Blade area (inches) = C x hp. C is a constant whose value depends on "speed of advance" which, in our case, is approximately 5 knots. If the hp were 3 hp, then the blade area would be equal to 15 square inches.

We will see that the blade area of a 12 inch, two-blade sailor prop (the off-the-shelf propeller with the smallest blade area available) is 27 square inches which is more than adequate.

Cavitation, where air bubbles get trapped in the rotating prop, is sometimes a problem when the blade area is too small and the shaft rpm's are too high. But, with shaft rpms of 800 to 1000, we have plenty of leeway before cavitation can create any difficulty.

It is informative to know how the blade area is calculated. Gerr tells us that a ratio is used to calculate the blade area of various types of propellers:

> The ratio for a two-blade sailor propeller is 24%.
> The ratio for a standard three-blade prop is 50%.
> The ratio for a three-blade wide prop or a four-blade prop is 67%.

For example, the 12 inch sailor prop mentioned above makes a circle having an area of 113 square inches (6 x 6 x 3.14) and has a blade area of 27 square inches (113 x 0.24). A 10 inch standard three-blade prop makes a circle having an area of 78 square inches. It has a blade area of 39 square inches.

Expected Results from Outboard Installations

The data provided above in the charts and formulas applies mainly to inboard installations. Another way to get a handle on prop size for electric power is to compare it with the propeller size of tried and true outboard motors.

Outboard Motor Propeller Sizes

The chart below shows the propellers used as standard equipment on outboard motors of various sizes. They were selected from the outboards suggested for use with heavy boats with displacement hulls.

Stock Outboard Motor Propellers				
Motor HP		# of Blades	DiamxPitch	P/D
OMC	25 HP	3	9 1/4x7	.8
	30 HP	3	11 1/4x7	.6
	35 HP	3	11x9	.8
US MARINE	25 HP	3	10 1/2x7	.7
	35 HP	3	10 1/4x10	1.0
MARINER	40 HP	3	113/4x83/4	.7
YAMAHA	40-50 HP	3	12 1/4x10	.8

We know that propeller speed vs. power output is a cube function. This means that doubling the speed of the prop increases the power output by a factor of eight. If we assume that the props in the list above were selected for motors whose peak hp occurs at 5000 rpm and that the motors have a reduction gear of two to one, we can say that the prop speed is about 2500 rpm.

To compare these propellers with the one that is needed in an electric installation where the prop speed is 1000 rpm, we must divide the outboard hp by a factor of 16 (the cube power of 2500 divided by 1000). Consequently, the chart showing motors in the 25 to 50 hp range is used.

As we can see, the diameter range is 9 to 12 inches (the average being 10.8 inches), which is a little less than what we found on the inboard charts. The average P/D ratio is 0.78, which happens to be exactly the same.

Other Possibilities

Although the many formulas and charts we have described are very helpful, we have mentioned before that selecting the best prop for a particular application and boat is as much art as engineering. Trying a prop one size larger and one size smaller than the size obtained from the formula is a very worthwhile exercise.

Even after having spent much time and millions of dollars on computer simulations and other design efforts, the designers of ocean liners try alternate propellers before they are satisfied they have made the best possible selection.

Given a 3 hp motor running at 2000 rpm with a 2 to 1 reduction gear on 21 ft boat, I would start with a 10 or 12 inch prop diameter with an 8 to 10 inch pitch. I would then compare the results with that of the next larger and smaller prop in diameter or pitch. Measuring the current and voltage in each case should provide a good indication of whether the optimum size has been obtained. For a direct drive such as the one I used in the Rhodes 19 with the Etek motor a good starting point is where I had my best performance results: a 9x6 prop.

Conclusions

1. Charts and formulas are a good starting point for the selection of a propeller for an electric boat.
2. For best propeller efficiency:
    a) Use a two-blade prop with thin blades.
    b) Use a large diameter prop (larger than the standard prop from a 5 or 6 hp outboard motor) with a pitch to diameter ratio of about 0.8.
    c) The speed of the motor and the reduction ratio determines the prop speed. The lower the speed, the better the efficiency.
3. A good starting point is a 12x10 propeller with a reduction gear of 2 to 1. For a direct drive start with a 9x6 prop.
4. Trial and error is still the best way to finalize the selection of the prop size for a specific boat and motor.

CHAPTER 12

Batteries

Introduction

The lead-acid battery is always the first to be blamed in any discussion about the limitations of portable electric power. True, it has not changed much in the last 100 years. It is still a heavyweight, and it stores very little energy compared to fossil fuels. But some of the comparisons are unfair. For instance, when we compare the energy of fossil fuels with the energy stored in the battery, we fail to consider that the battery can store and restore this energy hundreds of times, as opposed to the one shot performance of fossil fuels.

And when it comes to pollution, it is the hands down champion of low emissions. Even after its demise it can be resurrected: in the US 97% of the lead acid batteries are recycled.

In spite of the billions that have been poured into research for a better solution to the electrical energy storage problem, the lead-acid battery is our best choice today for boating applications, and it will continue to be for some time to come.

All the details of the chemical reactions taking place within the lead-acid battery don't have to be understood, but an overview of its characteristics is helpful.

The lead-acid battery is a chemical factory capable of storing electrical energy. As such it is susceptible to temperature changes and to aging. Positive and negative lead plates immersed in a weak solution of sulfuric acid (not so weak that they won't burn a hole in your clothes) produce the chemical reaction that generates an electrical current when the battery is discharged. The process is reversible and the battery can be recharged by sending a similar current from a charger into the battery. Losses in the form of heat are incurred during the charging process: to charge a 12 volt battery, the charging current must be supplied at 14.4 volts.

We will look at various types of batteries and consider their size, weight, power and cost. Most useful in the boating application are the 6 volt golf cart batteries and the 12 volt deep cycle batteries used for lighting and refrigeration on boats.

The new types of batteries (Nickel Metal Hydride [NiMH] and Lithium ion [Li-Ion]) are designed for hybrid and electric cars. We will discuss their characteristics: weight, size, capacity and cost after a review of the lead acid batteries which, at this time, it is still the best bet for electric boats.

Car Batteries

The best known and most common battery is the car battery. Deep cycle batteries, which are used in marine applications and battery operated vehicles look very much like car batteries but they have substantially different characteristics.

Car batteries are designed to produce short bursts of very high current (200 to 300 amps) to run starter motors. They are kept fully charged by the alternator most of the time. When they are discharged, it is usually due to a malfunction of the electrical system and it takes a heavy toll on the battery's life expectancy. These batteries are designed for a maximum of 25 full cycles of charge and discharge.

Deep cycle batteries, on the other hand, have much heavier plate separators and are designed specifically to be charged and fully discharged many times. A good quality deep cycle battery can be cycled 300 times. The one thing it can't do as well as the car battery is provide large bursts of power needed to crank over a heavy engine such as large diesels.

Deep Cycle Batteries

To power electric boats, the deep cycle battery is the prime candidate. There are many different types of batteries, (the Trojan Battery Co. alone has 37 types of marine batteries) such as the newer gel-cell batteries, which are sealed and can be installed in any position, but the best value is still the standard golf cart battery. It has the maximum energy storage capacity for its size, weight and cost. A 6 volt deep cycle golf cart battery weighs about 60 lbs, costs about $1.50 per lb to produce a maximum of 220 ampere hours of power at a discharge rate of 20 amps.

Characteristics of Deep Cycle Batteries

We have seen in the boat tests that the discharge current to the motor was about 30 amps at a voltage of 48 volts to produce about 2 hp of continuous power. In selecting an appropriate battery for a boating application, it is important to understand the basic characteristics and the ratings of the deep cycle batteries. We will use the 6 volt golf cart battery and the size 27, 12 volt deep cycle battery as our prime examples.

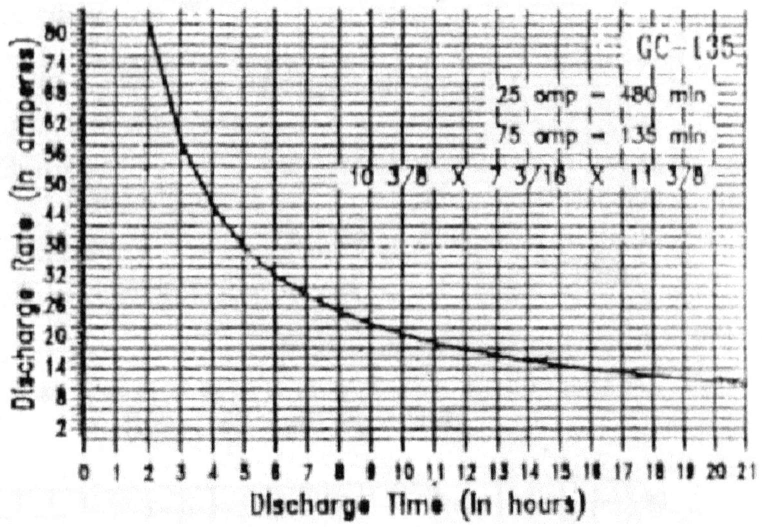

Figure 12.1 6 Volt Golf Cart Battery

As shown in Figure 12.1, the capacity of the golf cart battery is rated at two points: at a steady current drain of 25 amps and at a steady current drain of 75 amps. The power output of the battery is very different at these two points. As the curve above shows us, at 25 amps the battery is capable of supplying the current for eight hours. By multiplying these numbers together, we obtain the rating of the battery, namely 200 ampere hours.

At the 75 amp rating of the battery, the operating time of the battery is 135 minutes. This rating is incorporated in the model number of some batteries such as the GC-135. Notice that at this higher current rating, the same battery will only deliver 2.25 hours x 75 amps or 168 ampere hours. That's a 16% reduction in the power that the battery can supply at the lower current drain. **To obtain the maximum output from any battery, it is very important to discharge the battery at the slowest possible rate.**

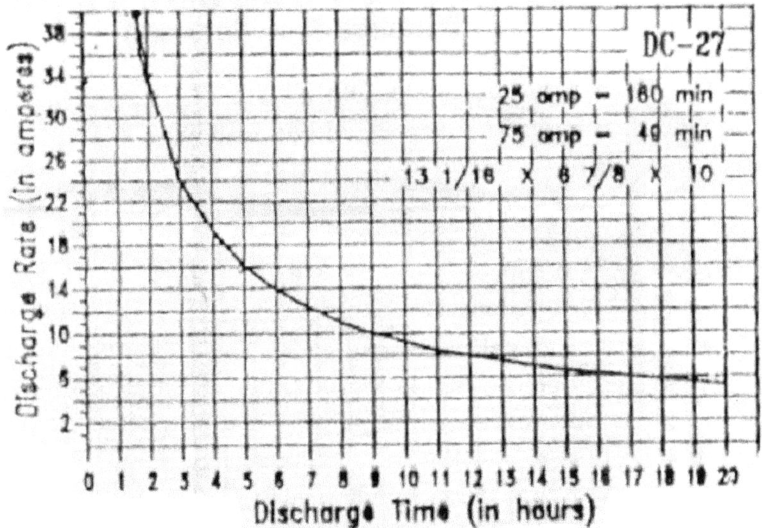

Figure 12.2 12 Volt Deep Cycle Battery

12 Volt Deep Cycle Battery

For electric boats requiring less range, such as a sailboat, the popular #27 size, 12 volt deep cycle battery is adequate. It weighs less than the golf cart battery (just under 50 lbs) and stores about 70% as much energy. Figure 12.2 above provides the performance data of this battery.

For example, at 25 amps, the discharge time is 2.8 hours (compared to eight hours for the golf cart battery--but remember that it has twice the voltage). In a boat operating at cruising speed, the drain would be about 30 amps with a discharge time of about 2.4 hours.

The Free Bonus

It would seem that if motor A (for AC) is 20% more efficient than motor D (for DC) at a given current drain, the range in miles should increase by 20%. You would think that if the range is 24 miles with motor D, it should be 29 miles for motor A. That would indeed be so if it were not for the free bonus that the batteries provide as reward for improving the efficiency.

Let's say that motor D draws 40 amps from the battery pack whereas motor A, being 20% more efficient, draws only 33.3 amps. Going to the curve shown in Figure 12.1, we find that a golf cart battery delivers the 40 amps of current for a period of 4.8 hours. But the same battery delivers 33.3 amps for a period of 6.0 hours.

At 5 knots, motor D will have a range of 5.0 knots x 4.8 hours or 24 nautical miles. But at the same 5 knots, motor A will have a range of 5 knots x 6 hours or 30 nautical miles, not the 29 nautical miles that might have been expected due to the higher efficiency of the motor alone. This bonus of 1.2 nautical miles, which adds about 5% to the 20% of motor efficiency improvement, comes absolutely free due to the characteristics of the battery. **A lower discharge rate produces more useable ampere hours of energy.**

The Bonus Miles

DC Amps	AC Amps	DC Hours	AC Hours	Gain In Hours	Boat Speed	DC Miles	AC Miles	Gain in Miles	Bonus Miles
50	43.5	3.6	4.5	.9	6.0	21.6	27.0	5.4	2.0
40	33.5	4.8	6.0	1.2	5.0	24.0	30.0	6.0	1.2
30	24.0	6.4	8.2	1.6	4.0	25.6	32.0	6.4	1.2

The chart shown above indicates the amount of free bonus energy that the battery will produce at three discharge rates. It assumes that the AC motor is more efficient than the DC motor by 15% at 50 amps, 20% at 40 amps (the example used above) and 25% at 30 amps. To provide an idea of what this means in terms of range, I'm assuming that the boat speed is 6 knots at 50 amps, 5 knots at 40 amps and 4 knots at 30 amps.

The chart shows the substantial improvement that can be obtained by powering the boat with a more efficient motor and draining the battery at a slower rate.

Battery Chargers

Battery chargers come in a variety of designs and prices:

The least expensive are tapering chargers. They are available for as little as $20.00 (for a 12 volt, 6 amp model) and can cost as much as $100.00 when features such as automatic shut-off are added.

Smarter battery chargers, which better match the profile of the battery's charging requirements, start at $100 and can cost as much as $400.00. The most expensive chargers will charge more than one battery at a time at rates up to 40 amps.

Golf cart battery chargers, which do a good job charging 36 and 48 volt battery packs, start in the $300.00 range.

Tapering Chargers

The inexpensive tapering chargers simply put out their rated charge rate and, as the battery is recharged and its voltage increases, the rate of charge decreases to a preset "float" current that keeps the battery fully charged.

Although not as sophisticated as the smart chargers, they do a good job because they charge the battery slowly. As we discussed in the section on "bonus miles," batteries last longer and generate more output (because less energy is wasted as heat) when they are discharged slowly. This applies to the charging process as well.

The Smart Battery Chargers

Experts now agree that the **fastest** way to charge a battery is with a three step process as shown in the graph below.

The first step is a bulk charge at a rate up to 40% of the battery's rated ampere hours and at a voltage of up to 14.4 volts (0.2 volts less for gel-cell batteries). It restores about 75% of the battery's total capacity in a minimum amount of time. The remaining 25% of the battery's capacity is restored at a decreasing rate between the six and eight hour marks while not exceeding a maximum voltage of 14.4 volts.

During the float phase, the voltage is decreased to 13.5 volts to maintain the charge without losing electrolyte from gassing.

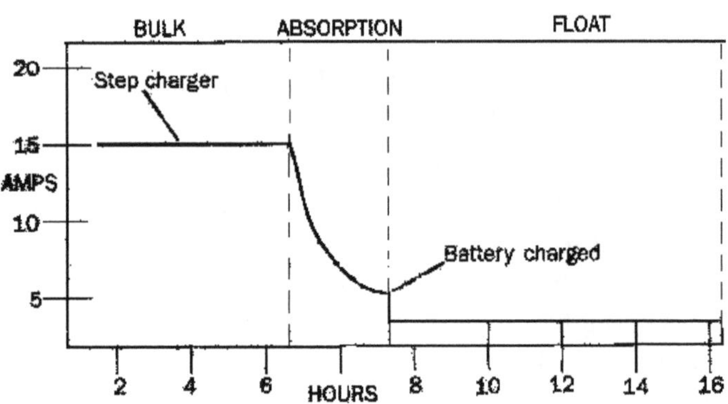

The Golf Cart Battery Chargers

The battery chargers described above are, with a few exceptions, 12 volt battery chargers. It would be far more convenient to charge the entire 36 or 48 volt battery pack at once. Golf cart battery chargers are designed to do just that. The ones that I looked at were tapering chargers (not smart chargers). They were designed to operate overnight thereby recharge the battery at a slow rate.

Battery Testers

There are three types of useful battery testers:

The hydrometer measures the density of the electrolyte.

The device used by gas station which puts a load on the battery while it measures the voltage.

The "fuel gauge" type of electronic device can be permanently installed in the console of a boat.

The Hydrometer

The least expensive battery tester (about $2.00) is a hydrometer. Some of the electrolyte is drawn into a plastic tube and, depending on the density of the electrolyte, one or more calibrated balls (or a calibrated float) rises in the tube and displays the amount of charge in the battery. (Mine only tells whether the battery is fully charged, half-charged or discharged.) This battery tester does work, but it is messy to use and the little balls tend to stick together or to the wall of the tube giving incorrect readings.

Exide Batteries sells a better quality hydrometer (for $6.00) that has a pointer and a scale with nine levels of charge indicated. This would be a good back-up tester to have around.

The Load Tester

The automotive testers apply a load to the battery (100 amps or more) and determine what happens to the output voltage of the battery. It is more of a diagnostic tool to determine whether the battery or the charging system is working properly, but it will tell you the condition of the battery. It is of little use to check the amount of power left in the battery pack on a boat.

The Fuel Gauge

The fuel gauge is based on the fact that a fully charged 12 volt battery has an output voltage of 12.6 volts and a 90% discharged battery has a voltage of 11.6 volts. (Gel-cell batteries read about 0.2 volts less). Expanded scale volt meters with a scale reading between 8 and 16 volts do an equally good job especially if they are calibrated in red and green to show the condition of the battery.

For the 24, 36 and 48 volt battery packs used in electric boats, the electric fuel gauge that reads like the fuel gauge in an automobile is by far the easiest to use. I have never used one because my trusty 50 volt voltmeter tells me everything I needed to know concerning the condition of the battery pack. It takes a little experimentation, but you soon find out that 50 volts (on a 48 volt system) is fully charged and 45 volts or less means the battery needs to be recharged.

Battery Safety

Lead-acid batteries generate explosive hydrogen gas while they are being charged so they need to be ventilated. Normal air flow is usually sufficient but a fan may be needed if the battery box is enclosed or receives very little air flow in a location such as under the floor or under the seats.

To avoid the problem altogether, gel-cell batteries can be used. They are sealed and require no maintenance. They can also be installed in any position. The original cost is higher, and they do not produce as many ampere-hours per lb as the standard deep cycle battery. A good discussion of the up-to-date developments in lead-acid battery technology as well as the pros and cons of each type can be found in the West Marine Boating catalog or in the book *Boat Repair*

Made Easy -- Systems published by Bristol Fashion Publications, Inc.

Batteries are heavy and need to be properly secured in the boat. Plastic battery boxes which can bolted in place are the best. But if there is inadequate room to lift the battery out of the box, a tray can be purchased or made from 1 x 1 inch strips of wood secured to the floor. A strap is needed to secure each battery.

The Nickel Metal Hydride Battery

The nickel metal hydride (Ni-MH) batteries are not new but they had not been mass produced until the advent of the Toyota Prius and Honda Insight hybrid automobiles in 2001.

The cells in the Ni-MH battery pack develop 1.2 volts each and are wired in series to develop 274 volts in the case of the Prius and 144 volts in the case of the Insight.

Each of the cells is only slightly larger than a "D" flashlight battery. Compared to the 15 pound weight of the 2 volt cell of the lead acid battery, the Ni-MH cell only weights a few ounces. Needless to say, there is no way that something as frail as the Ni-MH cell is going to turn over an automotive starter motor. Below, we compare the Prius battery pack with the lead acid battery.

The Prius battery pack is rated at 6.5 ampere-hours. Since we want to compare it with a battery which has a different voltage, we'll figure the capacity in watt/hours, namely 6.5 x 274 or 1780 watt/hours. This battery pack weights 87 lbs without the enclosure (mostly used for cooling) and the power electronics. With the needed accessories, it weighs 53.3 kg or 117 lbs

Two #27 lead acid batteries weigh about 100 lbs. They don't require much in the way of enclosure or electronics so we'll call their weight equal to the Prius battery pack. As the curve in figure 12.2 shows, these batteries will supply 25 amperes for 3 hours. With two batteries in series, the voltage is 24 volts. The number of watt/hours is therefore: 25 x 3 x 24 = 1800 watt/hours.

In actuality, because the Prius battery is so expensive (about $3000), in order to make it last through the eight year warranty period, it is never fully charged nor fully discharged. It operates at a depth of discharge (DoD) rate of 40%: from 80% of full charge down to 40% of full charge. This means that if we were to use the same DoD powering a boat, The Ni-MH battery would only have about half the capacity of the lead acid battery.

Because of the high output voltage this battery can provide 17 kw (62 amps at 274 volts or about 23 hp) to a motor for brief bursts of power. This would not be possible with two 12 volt deep-cycle batteries: at 24 volts, 23 hp would require more than 700 amperes. We should mention, however, that fast acceleration is seldom needed in a boat.

An Electric Airplane

I had the good fortune to work as a volunteer engineer on an electric plane (e-plane) project with a number of other engineers. Our leader was Jim Dunn, a brilliant IBM engineer who invented the laptop computer. (His detractors, at the time, kept asking him "who'd want one of those?")

Our goal was to build an electric plane to fly at the hundredth anniversary celebration of the Wright brothers' (champion do-it-yourselfers and my heroes) first flight on December 17, 2003. The e-plane would be totally high tech: fuel cells would generate the electricity for cruising (with battery power assist for take-off) and a composite fiber body.

The airplane selected was a modified *DynAero Lafayette III* an all carbon fiber airplane which seats two and weighed a mere 346 lbs. A number of grants and donations were used to procure the plane and the 71 hp, 300 volt, brushless DC motor from UQM Technologies.

Unfortunately, the fuel cell generator and its high tech fiberglass hydrogen tank (which, alone, would have cost over $100,000) never came close to being delivered on time.

Plan B called for the addition of a third Prius battery pack for the flight. I calculated that it would last about 12 minutes. (Not bad considering the Wright brothers first flight lasted only 12 seconds). But, as with most pioneering development projects, we did not get it done on time. We got to the point where the propeller rotated under battery power but the electronic controls were never finished. At the celebration, our e-plane looked very pretty with its electric motor and fuel cell **mock-up** but it never flew. (Photo below).

A $1.2 million replica of the Wright brothers' airplane sponsored by Ford Motor Co never flew either. Dec 17, 2003 turned out that to be a very rainy day at Kill Devil Hill causing the Wright brothers' replica to get stuck in the mud at the end of the 200 foot launching track!

Photo 12.1 The Modified Lafayette III ; 71 hp UQM Motor

But the idea of an electric airplane is far from dead. In 2008, *Boeing* flew a hydrogen powered fuel cell plane. Last year an Italian astronaut established a world speed record of 155 mph for a 100% electric airplane. That plane was not very different from our *Lafayette III* and I suspect that the new record will soon be broken. And, this year, Tom Peghiny's all electric ultra-light *e-Spyder* will be available for sale at a price of $24,000. A two-seater is on the drawing board. Progress marches on!

The Lithium ion Battery

The new "plug in" electric cars which can be charged overnight from an outlet in the garage will have lithium ion batteries. These batteries are lighter than the Ni-MH. They also have safety issues which are addressed within the cells and with the battery management software.

We have to assume that most of the main problems besides safety, such availability of the lithium and recycling of the batteries have been resolved because the US government is funding the construction of no less than 6 new battery plants as part of the American Recovery and Reinvestment Act of 2009.

I have no hands-on experience with Li-ion batteries but by reviewing Valence Technology's battery specifications, we get some insights concerning its performance.

Valence packages the Li-ion cells in the equivalent of a standard #27 series lead acid battery size which makes the comparison much easier. Their U27-12RT is rated at 130 Ah when it is discharged at C/5 (one fifth of the capacity rating) or 26 amps, it weighs 41 lbs.

Such a battery would provide about twice the output in ampere hours for the equivalent weight of a #27 deep cycle lead acid battery. For the same foot print, it would provide about 70% more output power. We have to assume that these batteries are far more expensive than the lead acid batteries, but cost aside, and according to the specifications, I see no reason why a direct replacement would not work well in a boat. Battery management software to control the charging and discharging rates and the operating temperature would have to be implemented.

Lessons Learned

I learned quite a lot about the new sophisticated high tech batteries while sorting out the wiring and charging and discharging the new NiMH batteries on the e-plane project. The main lesson is to forget about buying them in a battery store and installing them in your boat. These batteries need a number of safety devices to make sure that they do not fail or overheat. Several safety features are built in each individual cell, in addition, a very intelligent piece of "Battery Management" software must be developed for each application.

This software constantly checks the sensor information that is built into the battery pack. The temperature sensors provide the most important data. The software also determines the rate of charge and limits the rate of discharge. And, to insure the longevity of the battery, it controls the all-important depth of charge (DoD) mentioned above. Needless to say such an endeavor is not for the average do-it-yourselfer.

Conclusions

1. Lead-acid batteries, in spite of their many disadvantages, do a good job storing a day's worth of energy for boating power.

2. To take maximum advantage of the lead-acid battery's storage capacity, the battery power has to be released as slowly as possible.

3. Due to the battery's limited energy storage capacity, it is vitally important that all three components of the electric boat, namely the hull, the drive and the motor be as efficient as possible to reach hull speed and the best possible range.

4. The new batteries used in hybrids and electric cars are too expensive and are not well understood or proven to be considered by the do-it-yourself boater at this time.

As the new "plug-in" electric cars are mass produced, their characteristics will become common knowledge and many components such as the chargers and the battery management software should become readily available for electric boats.

5. The safety aspect of any of these batteries should be considered. They should be properly cooled, ventilated and securely anchored. The high voltage of the new types of batteries is also a concern in a salt water environment.

Part 3: The Build-It-Yourself Projects

Four build-it-yourself projects are described in the four chapters of Part 3.

Chapter 13. Describes how to build an electric outboard conversion using the leg of a 5/6 hp outboard motor.

Chapter 14. Describes how to install electric inboard power in a sailboat. It includes a good method to align the propeller shaft using the input power of the motor.

Chapter 15. Describes how to build a dynamometer.

Chapter 16. Describes how to build a solar power charger.

PART 3

Build It Yourself Projects

CHAPTER 13

Building an Electric Outboard Conversion

Introduction

Three chapters were left out of this edition: how to rewind a 3 phase AC motor, how to build an electronic motor controller and how to build a computer controlled motor controller. The feedback that I received was that these projects were too technical for this type of book.

The next four chapters describe four "do-it-yourself" projects. They have all been described in general terms in the previous chapters of the book. In the next several chapters, we go into sufficient detail to build the project. For instance, in the early chapters we described the tests done with an electric outboard. This chapter provides the details needed to build one.

I built these projects myself, and I'm an average do-it-yourselfer. One of my managers at IBM liked to say that he was an inspiration to his men. "They look at me", he would say, and they think "Boy, if he can do it, I can do it too."

Building an electric outboard conversion is a project for those who have a few mechanical skills and who would like to power a boat electrically. It can be a great winter project or family project at any time.

The goal is to build a reliable electric outboard with mostly used parts. Plan to spend \$500.00 to \$1800.00, depending on your choice of new parts, the type of speed controller and the size of the battery pack. The finished product will compare favorably with an electric outboard costing many times more.

Gathering All the Parts

The first step is to find the right outboard motor to modify. Some of the qualities to look for, besides price, are light weight, gear ratio of the lower unit and the condition of the unit.

As far as size goes, I like the 5 to 6 hp range. A Johnson/Evinrude outboard of that size manufactured in the last twenty years has a lower unit ratio of approximately 2 to 1, and the parts that are needed weigh about 20 lbs.

My first purchase was a very old (nearly forty years old) 15 hp Evinrude. It was certainly rugged enough but it weighed more than 30 lbs, and the reduction ratio was 1.75 to 1. Not a good choice. A better choice would have been a unit lighter in weight with a higher ratio.

Second Attempt

For my second attempt, I built an electric outboard using the leg of a 4 hp Evinrude. These motors were readily available and work quite well. After buying the motor, I was surprised to find out that it used a left-hand propeller. These props are not readily available. This outboard did not have a reverse. To run it with a larger right-hand prop, the shaft of the motor must turn in a counter-clockwise direction. This was not a problem for the electric motor, but the reduction gear was a little noisy in the reverse direction.

As we mentioned in the section on propellers, for best efficiency, it is advantageous to use a large propeller at low rpm. The 4 hp outboard has a reduction ratio of 2.42 to 1, which is very good, but the propeller shaft diameter is only 7/16 inches in diameter. This makes it difficult to adapt it to a large prop. I was able to build a sleeve to fit a 10 inch prop to the shaft. The 8 x 7.25 left-hand prop that comes standard with the outboard did not allow the electric motor to perform to its potential because there was too little pitch.

The 5 hp Evinrude

The 5/6 hp Johnson/Evinrude is a good compromise. It is rugged enough, not too big or heavy, and it has a ratio of 2.08 to 1. I like the older models that do not have the "thru the hub" exhaust and have a shear pin to protect the propeller. This arrangement makes it far simpler to fit a larger prop to the shaft, and there is a wider selection of propellers available for this less complicated shaft.

To get the most useable parts for the price, try to find an outboard with a blown power head. You will need almost everything else. If you can find a motor that was used in fresh water rather than salt water, it will save hours of labor when it comes time to disassemble the motor. If the available motor was ruined because it was submerged, make sure that it isn't corroded to the point that it can't be disassembled.

My best purchase was a 5 hp Evinrude with a blown head with all the parts except the cover for $25.00. It turns out that covers are hard to come by. Actually, they don't quite fit over the electric motor, which is taller than the power head of the gas engine (except for the Etek or Lynch motors). If you get a cover, a 2 inch shim will have to be installed on the interface plate to raise the height of the cover.

When it comes to covers, I don't have many good ideas. A custom cover can be built, of course, but it will look a little strange. Whatever is done, be sure to provide openings for ventilation and room for the electrical components. I never really tackled that problem. The only thing I used to protect the electric motor was a cover made of waterproof material with pull strings to keep it closed. It was not very professional looking but it worked.

More Things to Consider Before Buying the Motor

If you are going to buy individual parts, you will need everything from the handle on down, except the shift mechanism. If an acceptable cover is available, whether for that motor or not, take it. If the parts cost more than a $100.00, it might be better to look for an entire outboard motor.

One thing that will require some advanced planning is the matter of a long or a short shaft (20 inch or 15 inch). The method of joining the electric motor shaft and the outboard shaft affects the length of the leg. My experience is that it is easier to find an older short shaft motor in sizes less than 10 horsepower.

If the boat requires a short shaft motor, try to find a short shaft outboard. Should you happen to find a good deal on a long shaft motor, think about converting the long shaft motor to a short shaft. It is basically a matter of removing the 5 inch plug between the two lower sections of the leg. Since the gear shift will be locked in the forward there is no need to modify the shift controls. If the shaft is going to be cut for a Lovejoy coupler (method 1), either shaft length can be used. It will be necessary to obtain a short drive-shaft if the splines at both ends of the shaft are going to be used (method 2).

Summary of the Cost of the Main Components

Used outboard (blown power head) - $25.00 - $125.00
Couplers and Miscellaneous Parts - $25.00 - $50.00
Aluminum propeller - $25.00
Custom bronze propeller - $300.00 (new)
Controller - $50.00* - $300.00 (new)
DC Motor - $150.00* - $450.00 (new)
Battery Pack (three # 27 deep cycle batteries) $200.00

Battery Pack (6 golf cart batteries) $500.00
2 Relays (rated at 100 amp): start/stop and reverse: $100.00 (new)
* Used Golf Cart Parts

Total minimum cost $475.00
Total maximum cost $1825.00

Coupling the Shafts

The most difficult operations to be performed in converting a gas powered outboard to an electric are building and aligning the interface plate and joining the shafts together.

The two ways to connect the shafts together described here result in a different overall length for the outboard leg.

Method one, which uses a Lovejoy coupler between the motor shaft and the outboard shaft, requires cutting off part of the outboard's drive-shaft. The net result is that the length of the outboard leg does not change: it remains either 15 inches or 20 inches. It is the simplest way to couple the shafts.

Method two uses the spline of the outboard shaft. This adds 3 inches to the length of the outboard leg. A short shaft motor grows to 18 inches from 15 inches, while a long shaft motor grows to 23 inches from 20 inches. This is not necessarily a disadvantage because the larger propeller will run more efficiently if it is lower in the water.

Coupling Method Number Two

On the Carolina Skiff conversion, I was able to use a short shaft outboard motor for a boat requiring a long shaft because with coupling method number two, I ended up with the equivalent of an 18 inch outboard. When I replaced the 8 inch prop with a 10 inch prop, I added one more inch to the overall depth requirement making it 21 inches. It all worked out correctly by using an outboard motor bracket which I mounted on the transom. I positioned it down 3 inches to provide the proper clearance below the bottom of the boat.

The depth of the prop in the water is important. The top of the prop should be about 3 inches below the bottom of the transom. Be sure to make the necessary measurements based on the size of the prop that will be used and the method of coupling the shafts before buying the outboard.

A Few More Things to Check

When a good conversion candidate is found, be sure to check the reduction ratio. 2 to 1 or better is preferable. Also check the condition of the grease in the lower unit. If it is white, it means that there has been a leak. The "O" ring seals will probably have to be replaced. With the lower horsepower of the electric motor, number 30 oil is adequate to lubricate the lower unit and the gears instead of the heavier grease. It will reduce the friction and thereby improve the efficiency.

Basic Steps for an Electric Conversion

Once the motor has been procured, the fun can begin. The conversion of the gas powered outboard to an electric is broken down into the following six steps:

1. Disassemble and clean the gas outboard motor parts.
2. Remove unneeded items such as the water pump and lock the gear shift in forward.
3. Select an adequate propeller and modify the propeller shaft as necessary.
4. Build an adapter/interface plate to join the electric motor to the outboard leg.
5. Select a shaft coupler and modify the top part of the outboard leg to make room for it.
6. Install the electrical components and the cover.

Step 1
Disassembly

Most of the motor parts will have to be disassembled to get at such things as the crankshaft and the water pump. Sometimes these projects take longer than expected, so it is a good idea to keep notes and keep the various parts segregated in their own container. Keep one cardboard box for the power head with its own coffee can for the associated nuts and bolts and a different box for the lower unit with its nuts and bolts. Don't throw anything away yet! You'll want to paint the finished product, so this is the time to clean and lightly sand all the parts that will be used.

If the lower unit is dry or if the grease is milky white, it will have to be disassembled and the seals will have to be replaced. If the unit is in good shape, drain the grease and replace it with number 30 oil.

If the nuts and bolts are badly corroded, they will be difficult to take apart. I have never had any luck with WD-40 in these cases, but it doesn't hurt to try it. Applying heat to the area where the corroded bolt is locked in place always works. You will need at least enough heat to blister the paint job, but that can't be helped. Don't use excessive force or the bolt will surely break, creating even more work because the pieces will have to be drilled out and the hole will probably have to be re-tapped.

Some of the bolts, such as the ones holding the leg of the outboard to the power head, can be snapped off, since the power head will not be used.

Step 2
Removing Unwanted Items and Locking the Shift in Place

The water pump and the associated pipes connected to it will not be needed. Since they can cause problems if they run dry, they should be removed.

The shift mechanism should be locked in "forward" near the lower unit so that the shift handle can be removed and discarded.

The best way to lock the shift mechanism in "forward" depends, of course, on the motor selected. On the 5/6 hp Johnson/Evinrude, a simple bracket shown in the sketch below is easy to make. It is attached at one of the four screw locations previously used to mount the water pump.

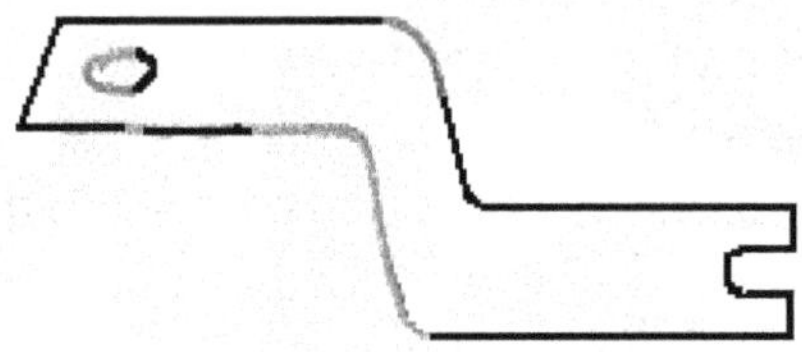

Shift Lock Bracket

Step 3
Selecting and Mounting a New Propeller

For maximum efficiency, the prop that came with the motor will not be adequate. Assuming that the electric motor will operate at half the speed of the gas engine, the propeller's output power with the electric motor will be one eighth of the power generated by the gas engine. A larger prop with more pitch will be needed to absorb the full power of the electric motor.

Selecting a Propeller

We have seen that the exact size of the best prop is not easy to calculate. It depends very much on the propeller speed, the type of boat and power of the motor. Some trial and error experimentation is necessary. A replacement prop somewhere in the 9x8 to 10x10 range is a good place to start.

Select a shear pin propeller rather than a splined shaft model, which would add another dimension of complexity to the job.

Look out for propellers with tapered holes. They cannot be drilled out because the inside bushing has been hardened. These inside bushings are vulcanized to a rubber bushing, which in turn is vulcanized to the inside hub of the prop. This construction makes it impossible to take the temper out of the bushing using heat without melting the rubber or to drill out the hole to a larger size. It is wise to avoid them.

If you feel sure of your propeller size, it is possible to order a custom prop with the correct hub and shaft size. This would be a brass two blade sailboat propeller used in inboard installations. However, they cost four or five times as much as stock aluminum outboard props.

Modifying the Leg

To make room for the new larger prop, the cavitation plate will have to be cut out. (It is not needed due to the low speed of the prop and of the boat.) The shaft diameter will, most likely, be too small and require a bushing to bring it up to the diameter of the propeller's shaft boring. It may also be necessary to extend the length of the shaft or reduce the size of the hub to make room for the propeller nut. Do not attach this nut to the bushing. Should the shear pin break, the prop and bushing would both fly off the shaft.

A little advance planning goes a long way when it comes to fitting a larger prop on the shaft with a minimum of work. A large selection of propellers is available. A good place to start is the *Michigan Wheel* catalog for outboard motors. Shear pin models in the 25 to 40 hp range are plentiful. Used props can also be found in the outboard motor repair shops.

After the electric outboard is assembled, make a quick check to see if the prop is about right, run the motor in a tank and measure the current going to the motor at full power with fully charged batteries. At 36 volts, a golf cart motor should draw about 50 amps.

Step 4
Building the Adapter Plate

The four mounting holes of the electric motor will not come close to matching the random location of the five or six bolt holes used to attach the power head to the top plate of the outboard leg. An adapter or interface plate has to be built with the circular bolt pattern of the motor and the bolt pattern of the power head.

Note that some of the bolts will be covered by the electric motor flange and will be inaccessible when the parts are joined together. This means two things: 1) the bolt heads will have to be countersunk, and 2) provisions will have to be made to keep these inaccessible bolts or nuts from turning as they are tightened. Good planning will keep these troublesome locations to a minimum.

Determining the Location of the Shaft

Before separating the power head from the leg of the outboard, it is important to determine the location of the drive shaft in its normal running position. This can be done by drilling two 1/8 inch holes at 90 degrees from each other and measuring the distance to the shaft with calipers. The holes should be drilled about 3.5 inches from the top of the leg. Some of the material at the top of the leg will be removed to allow the coupler to turn freely. The measurement holes must be drilled well below this point. The diagram below shows the measurement holes at a 90 degree angle from each other. During reassembly, after the shaft, coupler and electric motor are set in their final position, these measurements will insure that the shaft turns as true as it did before the modifications were made.

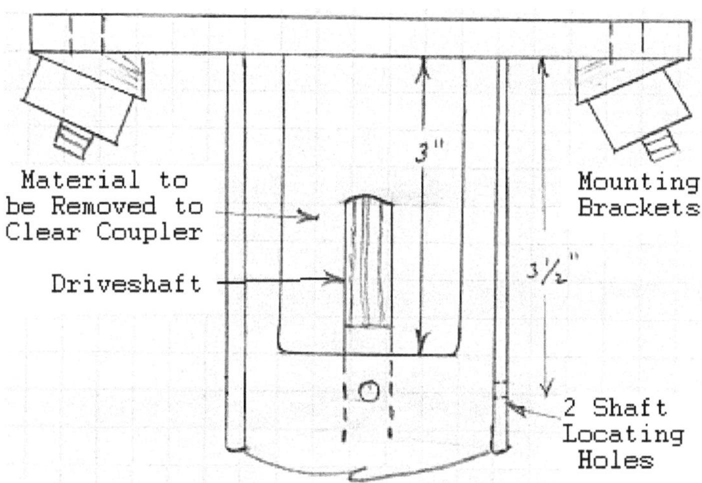

Shaft Locating Holes and Coupler Clearance

The Template

The power head can now be separated from the outboard leg, and a cardboard template can be made of the top of the leg. The one shown below was made by attaching the cardboard to the plate with double sided cellophane tape and, using a small ball-peen hammer, etching the edges and the bolt holes into the cardboard. Be sure not to cut out the middle area of the template because it will be used to locate the center of the drive shaft.

A template of the face of the electric motor is also needed. Simply draw a circle using a compass to represent the face plate of the motor on a sheet of paper (we'll call this the paper template as opposed to the cardboard template), locate the four mounting holes of the electric motor and draw a circle representing the shaft of the motor and its center.

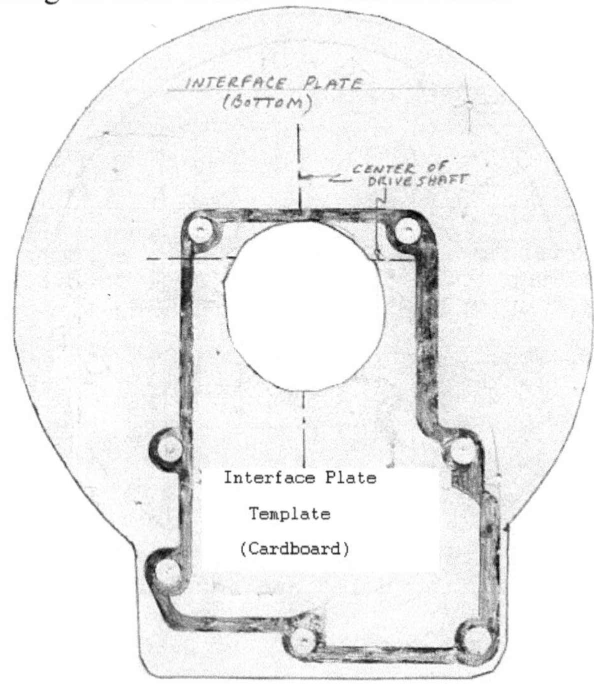

The next step is to position the drive shaft of the outboard leg in its correct position. By measuring the distance between the shaft and three of the mounting holes, the location of the shaft can then be transferred to the cardboard template.

First, the drive shaft must be shimmed with wood shims in its proper location using the dimensions obtained previously through the two 1/8 inch measuring holes. With the shaft locked in place, measure the distance from the edge of the shaft to the edge of the three main mounting holes. Add half of the shaft diameter to each of these measurements and transfer them to the cardboard template with a compass. Where the lines intersect is the center of the shaft. Using this center, drill a hole of the same size as the drive shaft in the cardboard template. When the template is positioned on the outboard leg with the shaft shimmed in place, the mounting holes should all line-up.

Double Checking the Measurement

One way to double check the shaft centering measurements is as follows: spin the shaft by turning the propeller. Without the power head bearing in place to make it turn true, the shaft will wobble as it turns. Stick a piece of masking tape around the shaft and mark four spots 90 degrees apart at the high and low points in the north-south direction and at the high and low points in the east-west direction. Measure these four distances with calipers and record them. Average the two readings in each direction and again lock the shaft in place accordingly with wood shims.

If everything has been done correctly, the measurements should correspond with the previous set and the cardboard template previously built should line up with the mounting holes when placed over the shaft.

At this point, the location of the two templates (cardboard and paper) must be fixed with respect to one another. First, cover the shaft hole of the cardboard template with masking tape and reestablish the center with the measurements from shaft to mounting holes. Then, with a pin, lock the centers of the two templates to one another. Rotate the electric motor template through 90 degrees to determine the location that presents the least amount of interference to the outboard leg mounting bolts. Make sure that all four electric motor mounting bolts are accessible.

The Interface Plate

I built all my adapter/interface plates with 1/4 inch aluminum plate stock. Scrap pieces can be obtained from welding shops or machine shops.

This is the time to decide what type of cover will be used so that the plate can be made large enough to accommodate the mounting hardware for the cover. It is also a good time to decide on the location of the accessories, namely the speed controller, the on/off solenoid and the reverse solenoid. Golf cart type motors are 7 inches in diameter and 10 inches high whereas the Etek motor measures 8 1/2 inches in diameter but is only 6 inches high.

None of the three electric motor conversions I built had a motor cover, so I don't have much advice to offer. Beside the footprint of the electric motor, provisions must be made for cooling and for the height of the electric motor. This will probably require 1 to 2 inch shims, which may have to be separated from each other to allow the air to circulate. Adjust the location of the adapter plate so that there will be room for the electronic control equipment (assuming that it will be located under the cover).

Finally, mark the location of the leg mounting holes using the cardboard template and drill and countersink as needed. At least three 5/16 inch bolts evenly spaced are needed to bolt the interface plate on the leg, but one or two additional fasteners won't hurt. The electric motor requires four 3/8 bolts.

Step 5
Coupling the Shafts

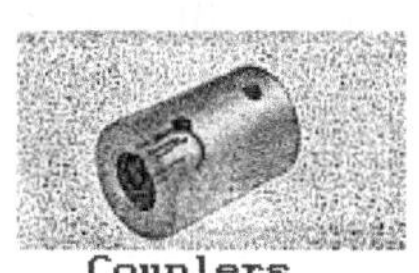

Couplers

Two ways of coupling the shaft of the outboard with the shaft of the electric motor will be discussed. The first method is to use a stock Lovejoy flexible coupling, and the second is to modify the end of the outboard's crankshaft (with the inside spline) to mate with the spline of the outboard shaft. Two types of flexible couplers are shown in photo above. The rigid coupler in the middle is the one that would be modified for coupling method number 2.

The Flexible Coupler Method

The first method is straightforward. The coupler comes in three pieces: one fitting for each shaft and a coupling spider between the two fittings. The L075 model is the smallest unit available to accommodate the electric motor's 7/8 inch shaft. Choose a second end fitting to match the outboard motor shaft (probably 1/2 inch). I found the Buna-N spider (as opposed to the more expensive one) adequate for the job.

The set screw provided to lock the coupling on the shaft is not the ideal engineering solution. At a minimum, the shaft should be drilled to provide more bite for a longer set screw. If that does not work, weld or braze the coupling to the shaft. The coupling used on the electric motor shaft is not a problem since a keyway is provided.

Cutting the outboard motor shaft to the correct length is, of course, vitally important. There should be no more than 1/32 of an inch clearance between the two shafts plus the thickness of the spider. Don't forget to add the thickness of the interface plate to the length of the shaft. Measure twice before cutting!

This coupling and the one described next are both 1.75 inches in diameter, which is about 1 inch more than the diameter of the outboard's crankshaft. The crankshaft's clearance is less than 1/4 inch to the forward edge of the leg. Additional clearance has to be provided.

The previous sketch showing the 1/8 inch measuring holes, also shows the material to be removed in order to clear the coupler. While the "Sawzall" is handy, remove some of the unneeded appendages that may be in the way of the electric motor's mounting bolts, such as the reverse mounting mechanism that is no longer needed.

Another handy tool is a small belt sander. It does a good job smoothing out the aluminum parts that have been hacked away with a saw.

The Second Coupling Method

The second method of coupling the two shafts uses the entire outboard shaft (no need to cut it) with the spline that fits in the power head crankshaft.

A coupling is fabricated from the end of the crankshaft as follows: the power head must be disassembled and the end of the crankshaft must be cut off. You will find that the crankshaft is hardened and can't be cut without removing the temper. This is easily done by heating it until it is cherry red with a propane torch and letting it cool.

The end of the crankshaft that was cut off is then inserted into a rigid coupling with an inside diameter equal to the electric motor shaft (most likely 7/8 inch). A rigid coupling is available from W.W. Grainger for about $14.00. It comes with a keyway. My crankshaft end was a bit less than 7/8 inch, so I wrapped it in aluminum foil to make it fit snuggly before welding it in place. Built in this manner, the coupler costs about $40.00, which is about twice the cost of the Lovejoy coupler but it is much stronger.

Adding a 3 Inch Extension to the Leg

The job is not quite finished. When the full length of the outboard shaft is used, the body of the outboard leg needs to be 3 inches longer (the length of the coupler) than the standard 15 inch leg. A 3 inch plug has to be fabricated and inserted between the top and bottom sections of the outboard leg.

To be sure, this job can be done many different ways. I used six pieces of 1/2 inch thick acrylic plastic. Using a cardboard template (shown below) of the junction between the two sections of the leg, I scribed and cut out six pieces of 1/2 inch plastic. After drilling out the mounting holes, the entire leg can be reassembled with four 3-1/2 inch long, 5/16 stainless steel bolts. A little sanding with the belt sander will contour the plug perfectly. See the Photo 5.3. The spaces between the six acrylic pieces do not have to be waterproof and gaskets are not needed.

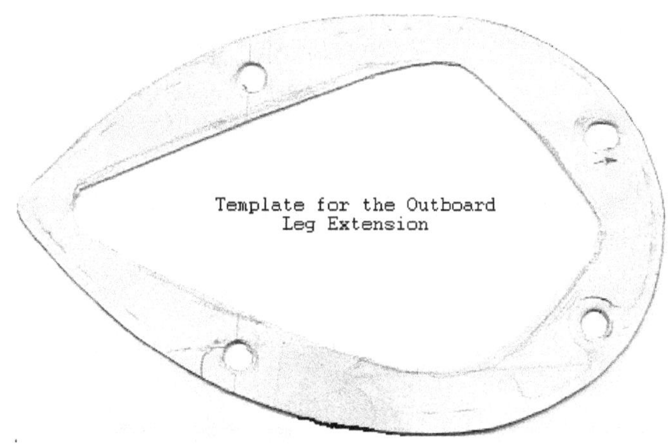

The final product is a leg 3 inches longer than a 15 inch outboard leg. It can be used on a short shaft transom or it can be mounted on an outboard motor bracket and the bracket can be adjusted up or down to replace either a long shaft or a short shaft outboard.

Step 6
The Electrical Accessories

This section describes the electrical devices needed to operate the Etek motor or the golf cart motor assembled in Step 5. This section covers how to turn the motor on and off; operate the motor in forward and reverse; and provide speed control. Three methods of providing speed control are discussed as well as the pros and cons of each method.

Method 1: Changing the Battery Voltage

Method 1 is the least expensive. It involves selecting a lower voltage from the battery for the slow speed. Three solenoids are needed: two to turn the motor on and off and a double pole, double throw solenoid to reverse the motor.

The main disadvantages of this method are: there is only one low speed and the need to recharge the battery with individual chargers for each group of batteries. A wiring diagram is shown below.

You might wonder why more battery taps could not be connected to the motor for additional speeds. That can be done, but it requires a more complicated switch to prevent two taps from being connected at the same time. In the diagram below, a single pole, double throw speed control switch is used to activate each of the two solenoids. I have shown the low speed lead connected to the 36 volt tap of the battery. If a slower, low speed is desired, this lead can be connected to the 24 volt tap instead.

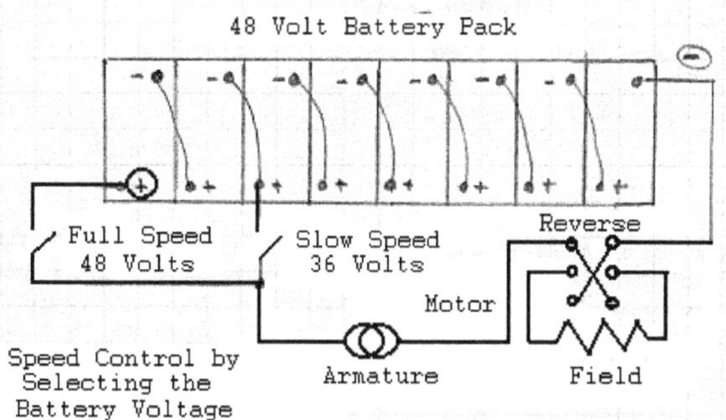

Using this method, only one solenoid can be activated at any one time. If both were closed at the same time, a destructive short circuit across two 6 volt batteries would result. A custom made rotary switch with "break before make" contact closures could be used to select additional battery taps.

At the designer's option, the electrical accessories can be located near the battery or near the motor.

Method 2: The Golf Cart Resistor Method

This method of controlling speed and motor direction involves using the old golf cart equipment that performed the same functions. I say "old" golf cart equipment because newer golf carts use electronic speed control devices. If you bought a used golf cart motor and acquired the controls at the same time, this method is worth considering. It involves using heavy-duty resistors to control the speed of the motor. It works perfectly well, but the heat that is generated by the resistors is wasted energy. If a prop is selected so that the motor operates at full power most of the time, this is a very inexpensive choice.

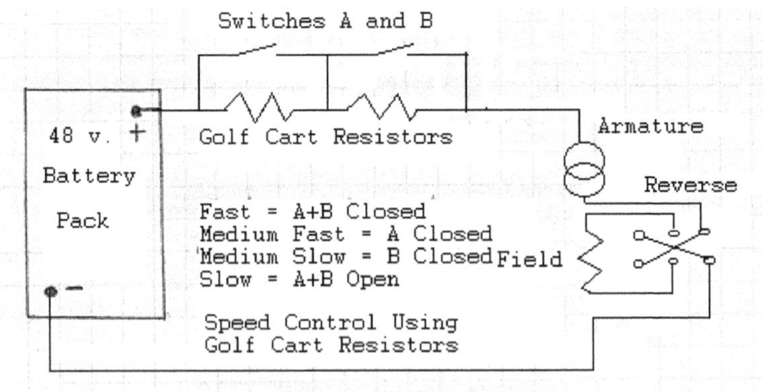

As the diagram above shows, the two solenoids controlling switches A and B provide four speeds: slow, medium slow, medium fast and fast. The reverse function and the motor on/off function are provided by the golf cart control switch. The resistors get very hot, so they need to be ventilated and kept out of harm's way. Heavy duty wiring is needed for this method.

Method 3: Electronic Controller Method

With this method, the two battery wires can be brought to the motor and the reverse and speed control can be done under the motor cover in a very neat and professional way.

Over the years, I bought two Curtis electronic motor speed controllers. One was rated at 200 amps, and the other was rated at 300 amps. I found that the 200 amp controller was perfectly adequate for the Etek or the golf cart motor. Two solenoids are also needed: one for the on/off function and one for the forward/reverse function. Together these parts cost about $400.00 to $500.00.

The main attraction of the electronic controller is that the motor speed is continually controllable from full speed to less than idle. As we discussed, the speed control is accomplished using pulse width modulation (PWM is described in Chapter 9), which effectively makes the motor think that the battery voltage is reduced. Although the motor can't tell the difference between PWM and a series resistor that also reduces the battery voltage, the advantage of using the PWM technique is that the unused power is not wasted as heat. This results in a greater range from the same size battery pack.

A wiring diagram of the Curtis controller is shown below. Note that pin A2 is not connected. This terminal is used for motor regeneration (charging the battery when the motor is forcibly slowed down). In a boating application, this feature would not provide any significant benefit.

The speed control is simply a 5000 ohm potentiometer that can be bought at Radio Shack. The on/off switch, which controls the solenoid, is an ignition type switch with a key.

The coils of the on/off solenoid and of the reverse solenoid should operate at the battery voltage of 36 or 48 volts. Solenoids rated at this voltage are not easy to find (most are rated at 12 volts) but some golf cart dealers do carry them. The Internet is also a good source for power contactors and double pole, double throw relays with 100 amp contact rating.

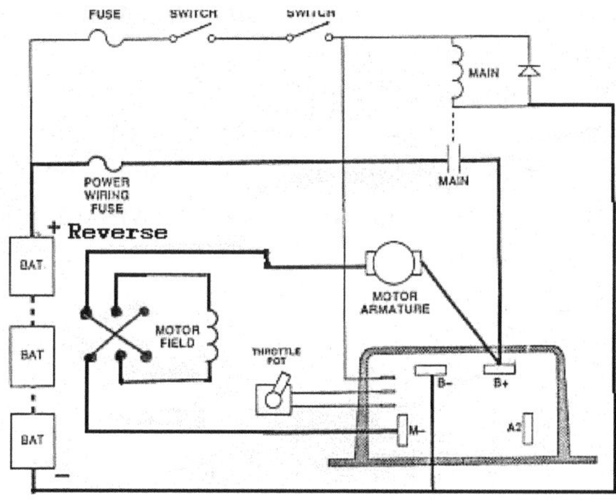

Additional instrumentation for the circuits above consists of a voltmeter and an ammeter. With a little experience, it is easy to tell the remaining charge in the battery from the output voltage under a load. When the voltage drops from 48 to 44 volts, for example, the charge is down to a quarter or less. The voltmeter is connected to points B- and B+.

The ammeter is very useful to determine which propeller does the best job and to obtain the best cruising speed under different weather conditions. The shunt is connected in series with the battery supply at the fuse or the main switch. By multiplying the voltage by the current, the input power to the motor can be determined.

Summary

Converting an existing outboard motor to an electrically driven outboard is a great winter project requiring some planning, patience and a few mechanical skills. The finished product is a quiet, powerful and dependable outboard motor with instant start capable of moving a 20 ft or larger boat at a surprisingly good clip.

For the antique motor buffs, this could be a way to revive some old outboards with power heads that are beyond salvage. It would certainly be amazing to see a boat with an antique outboard power its way forward without the usual dense cloud of smoke.

CHAPTER 14

Installing an Electric Inboard Power Plant

After spending a summer using a 2 hp DC motor attached to the 4 hp Evinrude outboard leg, I thought I could improve two aspects of my electric boating with *Sunny*. First, I thought I could improve the efficiency of the drive by increasing the size of the propeller while reducing its speed. Second, I wanted to improve the maneuverability of the boat. With the electric motor either in the well or tied on an outboard bracket, the power was astern of the rudder. When navigating in a narrow river, with the wind and current not cooperating, it was difficult to make a U turn without resorting to turning both the rudder and the motor.

An Inboard for *Sunny*

The answer was to convert *Sunny* to an inboard electric powered boat. With the prop in front of the rudder, the maneuverability would be improved and the prop could be increased in size and driven at a slower speed.

The plan was to keep the rudder in place but to cut out part of the skeg to make room for the prop. A horizontal cut would also be made in the skeg to accept a 2 inch fiberglass tube to hold the stern bearing and the propeller shaft.

Photos 4.1 and 4.2, showing the outside and the inside parts of the inboard installation, provide a good overview of the project.

Shopping for Parts

I went shopping for the parts and bought everything new except for the prop and the propeller shaft. The new parts were:

4 feet of 2 inch fiberglass tube.

A stern Cutless bearing for a 1 inch shaft with an outside dimension of 2 inches to match the interior size of the fiberglass tube.

A stuffing box for the 1 inch shaft.

A flexible rubber hose to connect the fiberglass tube to the stuffing box.

Miscellaneous clamps and fiberglass material to install the 2 inch pipe and to reconstruct the skeg.

These parts cost about $195.00.

I found a very good deal on a good used 12 x 10 inch brass sailboat propeller for $40.00 (a new one cost about $250.00). But I got ripped off on the 1 inch shaft that I bought at the same place for $70.00. Although I spared no effort to make sure that it was straight, it turned out to have a slight bend. I had rolled it on a flat surface and twisted it between two other shafts but still did not detect the defect. My advice is to make sure that whoever sells you a used part has a return policy. I had bought the shaft in Florida, so I was out $70.00.

Fortunately, I found a used, guaranteed straight, stainless steel shaft for $50.00 (a new one with the machining needed to fit a prop would have cost about $300.00). The other parts needed for the inboard installation were a pillow block bearing and the pulleys and belt. They cost about $50.00.

I was able to machine a 1/4 inch keyway on the shaft for the 6 inch drive pulley myself.

Mistakes

Besides the bent shaft, I made two other mistakes. By reaching through the openings under the seats, I was able to install all the parts without cutting an access hole in the floor of the cockpit. That was a bad idea. I should have cut an opening about 10 x 20 inches and installed a waterproof, non-skid inspection hatch. It would have been much easier to reach the motor mounts and the shaft bearing adjustments and shims.

I had replaced the cockpit floor of this boat with 2 inch strips of mahogany and could not get myself to chop it up. But there were too many adjustments to be performed to align the shaft and adjust the motor pulleys and the belt tension. A good access panel was needed to reach all these adjustments. For $65.00, I could have saved countless tedious hours of work and obtained better results from the inboard installation.

I also underestimated the torque of the motor. I thought that a 1/2 inch “V” belt would handle the power of the motor. I was using large pulleys (6 inches for the large shaft pulley and 3 inches for the motor pulley). The torque was too much to keep the belt from slipping after it warmed up. Possibly an idler pulley arrangement that kept the belt tight might have worked. But if I had to do it over, I would use a cogged belt and the pulleys to match. They are expensive, but they would do a much better job.

Pushing the Boat Along

The force created by the propeller along the longitudinal direction of the shaft is the force that pushes the boat through the water in forward and pulls the boat backward in reverse. This force, in the order of 50 to 100 lbs, has to be transmitted to the hull. The power transfer takes place at the pillow block bearing. I installed heavy duty collars on each side of the bearing to transmit the forward and reverse axial forces to the pillow block bearing.

Possibly, a better solution would have been to install a single large ball bearing in a center hole between the end of the shaft and a backing plate to transfer the axial force to the boat with less friction and more efficiency.

Results of the Inboard Installation

Overall, the results of the inboard installation were excellent. The best part was the excellent maneuverability resulting from the propeller wash hitting the large rudder. It is one of life's small pleasures to have a boat respond quickly and predictably to the turn of the wheel.

The noise from the inboard installation was a bit more noticeable than from the outboard but well within an acceptable range. Shock mounts for the motor would probably alleviate this minor problem.

As far as the efficiency goes, it was basically the same as that of the outboard configuration. Exact comparisons were difficult to make on the water. From day to day, the changes in the wind, currents and wave action were sufficient to make differences of a few tenths of a knot which are difficult to detect.

The gains in efficiency made by the larger prop were probably offset by losses in the belt drive, the seal around the shaft and the larger shaft bearings. The propeller angle might also have had a slight negative effect.

As we saw in Figure 4.1, the overall results obtained from the inboard and outboard configurations were almost the same.

All in all, from an aesthetic and operational point of view, I much preferred the inboard electric drive.

The Rhodes 19 Inboard

Chapter 6 described the installation of the Etek motor in the Rhodes 19 sailboat. Photos 6.3 and 6.4 show the very simple and straight-forward inside and outside installations.

The parts needed, starting with the motor towards the prop were:

1. An electric motor. The original Etek motor is now available as a direct replacement under the names: Etek-R, Etek-RT, ECM-R and ECM-RT (I understand that some of the original motors had heat issues so, it is best to stay away from those).
2. A solid shaft coupler. I recommend using the one piece clamp type ($30) which had a very tight fit on the 7/8 inch shaft. *Grainger* also sells a less expensive solid coupler (set-screw type), it has a looser fit which is very useful for preliminary alignment of the shaft, but not recommended because it causes more vibration than the clamp type.
3. A stock 7/8 inch replacement stainless steel shaft 4 feet long, with all the standard machining work done. I bought mine at Boat US (which has since merged with West Marine).
4. 24 inches of fiberglass tube with an outside diameter measuring 1½ inches. Since a rubber hose attaches to it, the outside dimension is not critical.
5. 6 inches of rubber hose to connect the fiberglass tube to the stuffing box.
6. A stuffing box for a 7/8 inch shaft.
7. A strut of the type shown on photo 6.4 with a cutless bearing for a 7/8 inch shaft.

The cost of these items is about $500 for the motor, $300 for the machined shaft and $300 for the rest of the parts.

Before the motor installation can begin a motor mount has to be fabricated for Etek motor. When I did this work, seven years ago, I could not find one. While searching the Internet today, I found them to be equally scarce, fortunately, one can easily be fabricated from ¼ inch aluminum.

Photo 14.1 shows the base which measure 5 x 7 inches and the two uprights which are welded to the base. The critical dimension is the distance between the 2 uprights which is 3 ¾ inches. The curved sections have a diameter of 4 1/2 inches for the front upright and 5 inches for the rear upright. The front mounting holes are drilled to accommodate two 3/8 inch bolt The back holes accommodate two 10mm machine screws. Two 10mm screws, 1 1/8 inch long, are needed to replace two original 10mm screws, 5/8 inch long, in the back of the motor.

An opening 3 x 3 1/4 inches is cut out of the bottom plate to allow the motor to be mounted as low as possible. When this is done, the mounting holes in the uprights are located 1 7/8 inches from the bottom of the base plate. The front holes are 4 1/8 inches apart. The back holes are 4 inches apart. The rear part of the body of the motor is flush with the inside part of the upright so, do not weld in this area.

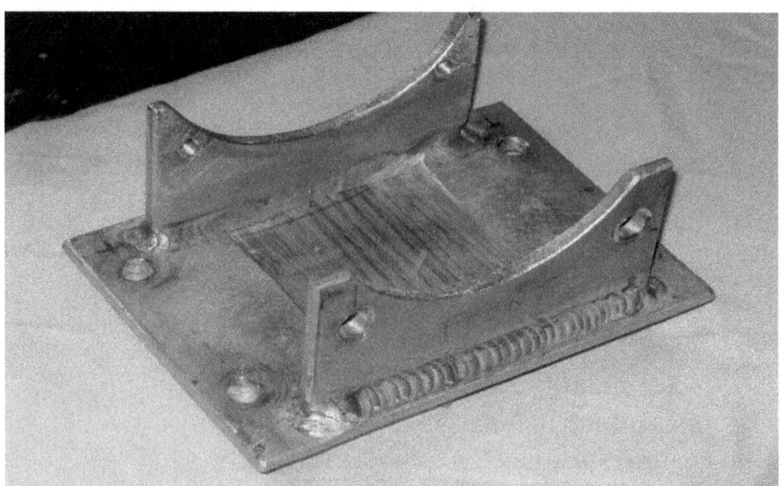

Photo 14.1 Motor Mount for the Etek Motor

Installing the Inboard in the Rhodes 19

I installed the shaft along the center line of the hull with the electric motor base just astern of the centerboard trunk. We know that a single shaft boat with a right hand prop has a natural tendency to go to port but I did not attempt to compensate for this condition with the shaft angle. For the motor base, I used an 8 inch piece of pressure treated 2 x 6 lumber which I cut at a 15 degree angle to fit the contour of the bottom of the hull. It can be either fiberglassed or bolted to the hull. The wood base brought the center of the motor shaft about 4.5 inches from the bottom of the hull and approximately at the correct angle for this boat.

Next was the installation of the strut. As the picture shows, the front part of the strut base had to be cut into the center part of the hull in order to obtain enough angle for the short four foot driveshaft. Getting the angle just right is a matter of trial and error between the angle of the motor and that of the strut. The motor should be as low as possible so that it does not intrude above the floor boards and keeps the shaft angle low. Struts with adjustable angles are also available if the angle is too difficult to obtain with a stock non-adjustable strut.

Cutting the Hole for the Shaft

Although the stuffing box is attached to a flexible hose to the fiberglass pipe, it still needs to be carefully centered over the shaft. The reason is that the marine hose is 5/16 thick and very stiff. To center the shaft properly in the middle of the fiberglass tube, hose and stuffing box, I assembled the three pieces, then I wrapped many layers of electrical tape around the shaft so that the stern end of the pipe would just fit over the tape. At the other end of the assembly, I wrapped fewer layers of tape on the shaft so that the stuffing box would just fit on the forward part of the shaft.

The best location for the hole in the hull can then be marked and cut out for the fiberglass tube and stuffing box assembly. Finally, with the motor and strut in place and the fiberglass tube assembly centered on the shaft all these items can be preliminarily aligned in order to fiberglass them in place. Needless to say, all signs of paint, dirt and grease have to be sanded away for proper adhesion to the hull.

Electric Alignment

After the fiberglass pipe is secured in the hull, the shaft can be positioned in the strut on one end and through the stuffing box at the other end. It should line up pretty well with the shaft of the motor but at this time we can still rotate the rubber hose (which is not perfectly concentric) to improve the alignment. Mark the best hose location for future reference. The rest of the alignment will have to be done by adjusting the height and the angle of the motor on its base.

A very good rough alignment can be obtained by sliding a solid coupler from the 7/8 inch boat shaft to the 7/8 inch shaft of the Etek motor. The rest of the alignment must be done by inserting shims under the base of the motor at the four mounting bolt locations.

I made a replica of the inboard motor drive by mounting the strut, stuffing box and motor on my work bench. The idea was to measure the current to the motor under the best possible alignment and under a number of misalignments. The amount of time that the motor and shaft require to coast to a stop was also measured under the best alignment and various misalignments.

At 12 volts, the Etek motor with no load connected runs at 1200 rpm, draws 3.2 amps and coasts to a stop in 4 seconds.

The motor was then connected to the shaft with a solid clamp type coupler. With the best alignment of the strut, stuffing box and motor, the motor drew 3.9 amps and coasted to a stop in 3 seconds.

On the bench, I could not duplicate the water lubrication of the cutless bearing in the strut nor of the stuffing box. I gave these bearings a squirt of WD-40 before taking each of the measurements. Also, I could only estimate how tight the stuffing box gland had to be and I might have been a little light on that point seeing that my previous in-the-water readings were .5 amps more than the .7 amps obtained on the bench tests. I used ¼ inch flat washer as shims, they are, on average, one sixteenth inch thick.

Nevertheless, the results shown below clearly indicate the best shaft alignment.

Best alignment:	3.9 amps	3 seconds
Motor lowered 1/16"	4.0 "	3 "
Motor lowered 2/16"	4.4 "	3 "
Motor lowered 3/16"	5.6 "	2 "

The results obtained when the motor is mounted at the wrong angle are even more dramatic. After finishing the measurements shown above, I again aligned the motor to its best position. This time the best alignment reading was 3.7 amps. A shim was then removed underneath the 2 stern mounting bolts thereby increasing the downward angle of the motor. A second shim was removed also. The results are shown below:

Best alignment:	3.7 amps	3 seconds
Stern lowered 1/16"	5.1 amps	3 seconds
Stern lowered 2/16"	7.1 amps	2 seconds

The best in-the-water result that I obtained seven years ago with these same components was 4.4 amps, which is about 1 amp more than the no load current of the motor at 12 volts.

Another worthwhile check is to make sure that the readings taken on land or on a boat trailer correspond with the readings with the boat in the water where the hull is supported more evenly. I performed these tests by removing the prop and found no difference between the-in-the water and trailer tests.

Electrical Accessories

The electrical accessories described in step 6 of the previous chapter apply to the inboard installation as well as the outboard installation. Although more expensive, the Curtis controller (or equivalent) is recommended for an inboard installation.

Being more efficient, it requires fewer batteries to obtain the same range as some of the other methods of speed control. This is particularly beneficial for a smaller boat like the Rhodes 19 whose excellent results depend partly on the light weight of the boat.

Results of the Inboard Installation in the Rhodes 19

Overall, the results of the inboard installation in *Sunny II* were excellent. As we found with *Sunny,* the maneuverability resulting from the propeller wash hitting the large rudder was outstanding.

As far as the efficiency goes, this boat was far superior to any of the other electric conversions. As we saw in Chapter 6, with only three 12 volt batteries the range would be close to 20 miles at 6 mph. If I were to do it again I would use four 12 volt batteries (two in the bow and two under the rear deck). The range would be even greater and short bursts of speed up to 7 knots could be obtained.

CHAPTER 15

Building a Dynamometer

Introduction

For the experimenter, hobbyist or engineer who might be interested in developing a high efficiency motor, be it a DC, AC or permanent magnet motor, it will be necessary to test his or her work. If the motor is modified, "before" and "after" tests must be made. If the experiment is a new concept, such as the 3 phase AC motor described in chapter 9, the experimenter will have to compare its performance with the performance of available, off-the-shelf motors. A dynamometer is needed.

The dynamometer is a device capable of accurately measuring the output power of a rotating device at various levels of power and speed.

When the EPA states that a certain brand of automobile obtains a certain number of miles per gallon in city driving and highway driving, the cars are not actually driven around town or on the highway. Variables such as traffic, temperature and wind conditions would distort the results. Instead, the results are obtained by putting the car through a standard series of tests on a dynamometer. And, because these tests can be closely duplicated with each brand of automobiles, it is possible for the customer to compare the results and make a sensible purchasing decision.

Finding a Used Dynamometer

I realize that few people are in dire need of a dynamometer, but for motor experimenters or hobbyists they are a vital necessity.

Dynamometers are custom built for specific applications. They tend to be expensive and difficult to find on the used market. After an unsuccessful search for one, I decided to build my own. It turned out to be easier than I had anticipated.

Efficiency is defined as the ratio of the output power divided by the input power. For example, if the input power of a motor is 40 amps at 48 volts or 1920 watts and the output power is 2 hp, we can convert the 2 hp to watts by multiplying by 746 and dividing the resulting 1492 watts by 1920 watts. The answer is 78% efficiency.

The input power is easy enough to determine with an ammeter and a voltmeter, but to determine the output power we need a dynamometer.

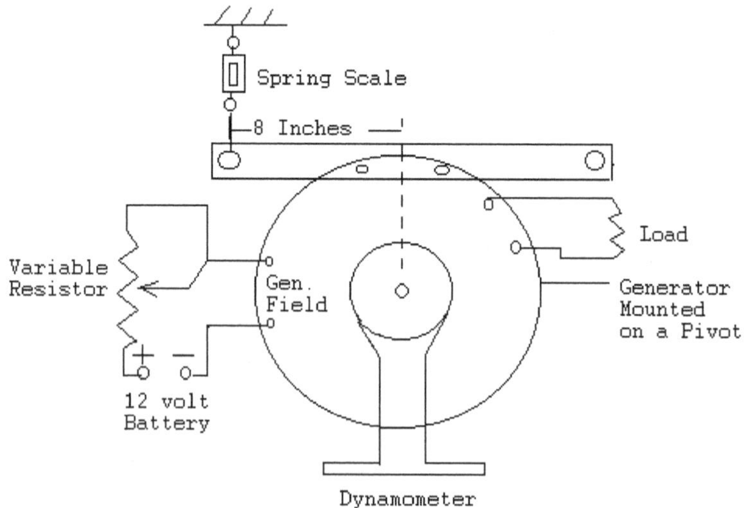

As we mentioned previously, the output power can be determined mechanically using a device known as a Prony brake. My efforts to build a practical device of that sort turned out to be a waste of time because the accuracy of the machine was deficient.

The output of a motor can also be determined by attaching a generator to the motor. The output of the generator can be measured in watts with a voltmeter and an ammeter. The problem here is to know the efficiency of the generator at each of the speeds and power levels used in the test.

The best solution is to connect a generator to the motor under test to absorb the power developed by the motor. By balancing the generator on a pivot in front and back, the torque produced by the motor can be measured. Knowing the torque and the speed is all that is needed to determine the hp.

The sketch on the previous page shows the mechanical configuration of the generator and the scale needed to measure the torque. The formula used to determine the hp is as follows:

hp (output in watts) = Pounds x rpm x K
Constant K for an 8 inch arm is 0.095
K is obtained as follows: 2 x 8 inches x 3.14 x 746 / 12 x 33000 (two times the radius in feet multiplied by pi times 746 watts divided by 33,000)

In addition to the generator (which can be an AC or DC device), two more pieces of electrical equipment are needed. The first is a resistive load for the generator (to dissipate the output power) and the second is potentiometer to vary the field current of the generator so that the load on the motor can be adjusted.

The spring scale is a good quality 50 lb fish scale.

Since the generator will not be used continuously, it can be somewhat undersize. To test a 3 hp motor, a 1500 or 2000 watt generator should be adequate.

Finding a generator, especially a used one, may not be easy. The ideal one would be an AC or DC generator, with a 2000 watt output at 1800 to 2500 rpm. An output shaft at each end to accommodate the pillow block bearings on which it will pivot would be a definite plus. If a 3600 rpm generator from a motor/generator set is used, it would be wise to get a larger size, say 3000 watts, in order to generate 2000 watts of power at the lower speed.

Building a Dynamometer

After doing a fair amount of unsuccessful searching, I resurrected an old World War II B-29 airplane generator I had bought on the war surplus market some fifty years ago. The plan had been to turn it into an arc welder. That project never really materialized, but I had kept the generator all these years and still had the coupler and a rheostat to control the field current. All I needed were two pillow block bearings for the pivot mount and a resistive load.

I found a pillow block bearing that fit perfectly on the shaft in the *WT* (Wholesale Tool) catalog for about $12.00. To mount the back pillow block bearing, I built a flat, 1/8 inch plate with four holes matching the shaft bearing cover. A short 1/2 inch shaft was then centered and welded to it, making the generator appear to have a shaft at each end. The shaft fit into the 1/2 inch bearing of the rear pillow block.

The rheostat that I used had a resistance of 4 ohms in 20 steps (0.2 ohms per step). The size of the resistor depends on the resistance of the field, but if a 12 volt battery is used, a good starting point would be a 5 ohm, 100 watt, wire-wound rheostat.

For the load, I used two of the resistors that came with my first purchase of golf cart equipment. Here again some experimentation is needed to find a proper load for the generator.

My ancient airplane generator worked equally well in either direction. I put more than 100 hours of testing on this dynamometer without any problem.

Photo 7.2 shows the dynamometer attached to the 2 hp motor under test.

The coupling, the pillow block bearing and the 8 inch arm can also be seen. I replaced the original 12 inch arm that I had installed with an 8 inch arm in order to get better readings on the spring scale.

CHAPTER 16

Building a Solar Battery Charger

For the fortunate boaters who have a slip with an electrical outlet or even the less fortunate who trailer their boat and can recharge their batteries at home, a solar charger would not be of great interest. Battery chargers that plug into the AC outlet are more powerful and less costly than the solar chargers. A top of the line 36 volt or 48 volt charger used for golf carts, capable of charging a battery at 10 amps costs about $400.00. Less expensive automotive 8 amp, 12 volt chargers costs about $40.00.

But, when a boat is on a mooring, there are only two practical choices to recharge the batteries: a wind generator or solar panels.

Wind generators are very powerful in strong winds. They can generate 15 amps in 25 mph winds. But in average winds of 10 to 15 mph, the output drops down to 2 to 5 amps. Their main disadvantages are they only generate 12 volts, cost over $1000.00, are quite noisy and require special attention when the wind gets too strong.

Although I had no experience with wind generators, I decided to go with the solar panels because they could be configured for any voltage from 12 to 48 volts and seemed to be maintenance free.

Solar panels are not without disadvantages either. They require a large shadow-free area, and for an equivalent output, they are even more expensive than the wind generators.

Description of the Solar Panels

A solar panel is made up of many solar cells. These cells generally measure 4 x 4 inches (3 x 3 inch cells are also available). A 4 x 4 cell delivers up to 3 amps at 0.45 volts when illuminated with direct sunlight. Since the sun does not shine directly on the cells most of the time, the average output is closer to 2 amps. Of course, on a cloudy day the output drops even more: 0.5 to 1 amp is common. One saving factor is that even when the current drops down to a trickle the voltage remains close to its rated value. The battery continues to be charged albeit at a very slow rate.

Attempts are sometimes made to tilt the panels at an angle so that the sun's rays are perpendicular to the panel for a greater percentage of the time. In a boat that tends to bob about randomly, I don't think this is a practical endeavor.

Used Solar Panels

I was fortunate to spot a California company's advertisement in *Boat U.S.* offering used Arco 13 x 42 inch solar panels for $100.00 each (new they would cost about $400.00). These panels had apparently been used in a "sun farm" application because they were wired for maximum current at an output voltage of only 5 volts. By removing the parallel connections and connecting the cells in series, it was easy to modify the panels for a 15 volt output. I bought four of them and they all worked very well.

Life of a Solar Panel

Solar cells do not wear out and are usually guaranteed for ten years. They are very forgiving. They can be shorted or left open-circuited without damaging the cells. To produce enough voltage to charge a 12 volt battery (about 14.4 volts), thirty or more cells are connected in series. Such a panel measures approximately 13 x 42 inches. Several panels can be connected in series to charge battery packs having output voltages of 24 to 48 volts (four panels for a 48 volt battery pack, for instance).

The main thing to remember is that since the cells are in series with each other, the output in amps of the least productive cell controls the output of the entire panel (like the proverbial weak link in a chain). If, for example, four panels are connected in series to charge a 48 volt battery pack and the shadow from the mast covers one or two cells, the charging current will immediately drop from 3 amps to less than 1 amp.

A Sailboat with a Roof

I built two canopies incorporating solar panels for my sailboat. The first had three solar panels in series to charge a 36 volt battery pack while the second one had four solar panels: two sets of two panels in parallel to charge a 24 volt battery pack.

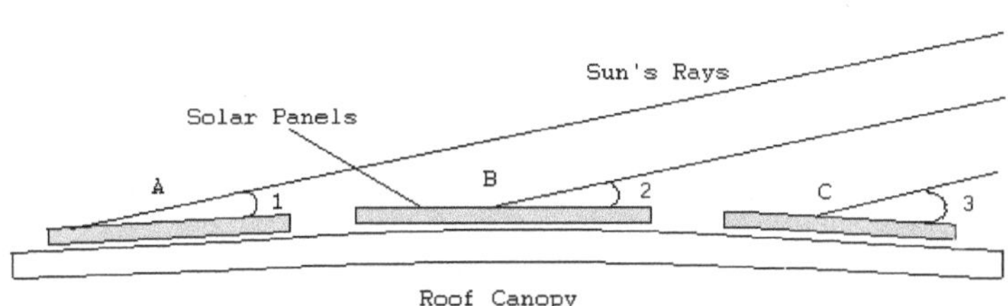

For aesthetic reasons, I wanted to curve the roof so that the middle of the roof would be about 4 inches higher than the sides as shown in the sketch above.

But, consider what happens when the sun's rays hit the panels. If the roof is flat, the rays would all be at the angle at which they hit panel B (angle 2). But with the curved roof, Panel C receives the rays at an angle closer to perpendicular, which is helpful, but panel A receives the rays at angle 1 which is shallower than the angle of either panel B or panel C. This reduces the output of panel A and, since the minimum output of the three panels controls the overall output, no matter where the sunrays come from, the overall output is less than with a flat roof.

In view of this situation, I built a flat roof to mount the panels. Besides being ugly, an unforeseen problem occurred. The boom that swung a few inches above the roof always cast a shadow on some part of one panel thereby reducing the output of all three panels. To remedy this problem, I was forced to remove and store the boom after each use of the boat.

The 24 Volt Roof

The second roof was built to charge a 24 volt battery pack. Two panels were installed on the port side and two on the starboard side with as much empty space as possible in the middle where the boom's shadow would have darkened the solar panel. The roof was flat but the front and rear were finished with a 5 inch curved end piece that improved the looks of the canopy considerably.

Each side of roof frame was constructed with three pieces of 3/4 inch pine, 2/12 inches wide glued together and interlocked at the corners for added strength. The roof was supported by four posts. They were fabricated from 1 inch aluminum tubing with 3 inch x 3 inch bases welded on each end. I found that the roof had too much movement from side to side and forward and back, even with the bases securely fastened. To provide added strength, I tied the front of the roof to the mast with two small brackets.

With two sets of panels in parallel, the charging current doubled to 6 amps at midday. Moreover, even when the boat swung around at its mooring, the chances of having both sets of panels in a shadow was greatly reduced, thereby improving the charging performance substantially.

Photos 2.3 and 3.2 show the finished canopies for a 36 volt and a 24 volt installation.

Installing the Solar Panels

The solar panels are installed in a groove in the roof frame (or any other frame) the same way as a windowpane is installed in a window frame. A bead of sealant (preferably marine poly-sulfide) is spread on the frame below the glass panel. Another bead is laid down above the glass to seal it to the edge. I think the sealant is sufficient to keep the panel in place, but I added a strip of wood over the edge of the panel to make sure it would not fly away in a strong wind.

The wiring from the solar panel to the battery should be fused (10 amps) and include an ammeter (0 to 5 amps for one set of solar panels). An on/off switch and a series diode should also be installed in the positive connection. The purpose of the diode is to prevent current from feeding back from the battery to the solar panel. A small amount of current (in the order of 100 milliamps) will flow into the solar panel at night without this blocking diode. A 10 amp diode rated at 50 volts or more from Radio Shack will do the job nicely.

It is possible to overcharge batteries, but the rule of thumb is that a battery can stand a continuous trickle charge of 2% of the rated ampere hours of the battery without sustaining any damage. In the case of the golf cart batteries that would be 4.4 amps. With solar panels, this is not a likely occurrence for an extended period of time. When I felt that the battery might overcharge, I simply turned off the switch.

Sealing All Connections

The wire connections must be completely sealed from the elements. With the salt air acting as a conductor, bare wires and connections will corrode and disintegrate in a few months. I mistakenly thought that soldered connections would be impervious to the weather but they soon disintegrated, too. **Every connection must be sealed.**

Performance of the Solar Panels

A useful rule is that a solar panel continuously directed towards the sun generates 50% of its rated wattage in ampere hours each day. But, if it is randomly oriented towards the sun, as it would be on the roof of a boat, it only generates 25% of its rated wattage in ampere hours in one day. The 42 x 13 inch Arco panels used on *Sunny* were rated at 46 watts; therefore, 12 ampere hours of charge was expected each day from each set of panels.

With two sets of panels in parallel, 24 ampere hours are generated each day at 24 volts. To fully charge the 220 ampere hour batteries at 24 ampere hours per day takes eight or nine days.

Another way to look at the performance of the solar cells is to consider a motor requiring 2 hp of input power or about 1500 watts (approximately 60 amps at 24 volts). It takes about two and a half days of solar charging for each hour of operation. With a week's worth of charging, the boat can be expected to run about three hours.

Whether this is acceptable or not depends on your use of the boat. It surely would not be adequate for an avid fisherman. But for the average boater in the Northeast where a motorboat is used less than fifty hours per season, it would be more than adequate.

Sailboat engines are used even less than that. I can't remember using more than two or three tanks of fuel during a season. Assuming 15 gallons being used at a half gallon per hour, this figures out to be about thirty hours per season.

Overall Results

For me, the solar panels worked fine. I started the season with fully charged batteries and used the boat once or twice each week, sailing on the good days and motoring for two or three hours when sailing conditions were poor. I can only recall one day when the batteries got very low following some intensive testing of the motor.

Final Thoughts

Of the twenty-five or so boats that I have owned, equally divided between sail and power, *Sunny* and *Sunny II*, with their electric inboards, were my most enjoyable sailboats. They seemed to glide along so effortlessly and quietly under power. And, of course, the advantage of having the electric power available at an instant's notice really added to my sailing enjoyment.

Much more work needs to be done to make electric boating a popular reality. It's an ongoing process on which I hope to report again in the future. The new batteries and new electric motors provide exciting possibilities for electric boat propulsion. Meanwhile, dear readers, be good to each other and to our planet.

About the Author

Charles Mathys

Charlie Mathys was born in Brussels, Belgium and was brought to the US as a child but returned to Europe for his primary education.

At age 14, he returned to the US to stay. He learned to speak English while attending high school and by age 20, he had graduated from college obtaining a BS degree in electrical engineering from Northeastern University. In 1963, he acquired an MBA degree from Boston College.

After a 2 year stint in the US Army, he joined IBM at the very beginning of the computer era. He stayed at IBM for nearly 10 years before working for three small start-up companies doing computer research and development work hoping to find fame and fortune.

He finally settled down at Mitre Corp, a non-profit, "think tank" corporation doing consulting work for the Electronic Systems division of the US Air Force.

After retiring from Mitre, he combined his expertise in electronics and his love of boats to design an efficient electric motor for the propulsion of recreational boats. The results of his experiments are the subject of this book.

Several years later, he converted a minivan into a small camper. He published the design of this inexpensive RV in a book titled "My MiniCamper Conversion." For more information visit www.myminicamper.

He lives in Massachusetts and Florida with his wife. From there, they often visit the families of their three children and seven grand-children.

CPSIA information can be obtained
at www.ICGtesting.com
Printed in the USA
BVHW041513190721
612146BV00012B/644